I0101894

An Introduction to Romans
A Christian Missionary Letter

First Fruits Press
The Academic Open Press of Asbury Theological Seminary
859-858-2236
first.fruits@asburyseminary.edu
http://place.asburyseminary.edu/firstfruits

Asbury Theological Seminary
204 N. Lexington Ave., Wilmore, KY 40390
asburyseminary.edu
800-2ASBURY

An Introduction to Romans, A Christian Missionary Letter: A Formational and Theological Interpretation, by R. Jeffery Hiatt

Published by First Fruits Press, © 2014

Digital version at http://place.asburyseminary.edu/academicbooks/5/

The author(s) has granted permission to First Fruits Press to electronically publish this item for academic use. Copyright of this item remains with the author(s). For any commercial or non-educational use of the material, please contact the author(s) directly. First Fruits Press is a digital imprint of the Asbury Theological Seminary, B.L. Fisher Library. Its publications are available for noncommercial and educational uses, such as research, teaching and private study. First Fruits Press has licensed the digital version of this work under the Creative Commons Attribution Noncommercial 3.0 United States License. To view a copy of this license, visit http://creativecommons.org/licenses/by-nc/3.0/us/.

For all other uses, contact First Fruits Press:
859-858-2236
first.fruits@asburyseminary.edu

ISBN: 9781621711001 (print), 9781621711506 (digital)

Hiatt, R. Jeffrey (Robert Jeffrey)
    An introduction to Romans : a Christian missionary letter : a formational and theological interpretation / by R. Jeffrey Hiatt.
    viii, 155 p. : ill., fascims, map ; 21 cm.
    Wilmore, Ky. : First Fruits Press, c2014.
    Includes bibliographical references.
    ISBN: 9781621711001 (pbk.)
    1. Bible – Romans -- Commentaries. I. Title.
    BS2665.53 .H34 2014   227.107

Cover design by Kelli Dierdorf

An Introduction to
Romans

A Christian Missionary Letter

*A Formational and
Theological Interpretation*

by

R. Jeffrey Hiatt

*First Fruits Press
Wilmore, Ky
c2014*

Dedication

To God, without whom this work would not have been possible or had meaning;

To my children: James (JimBob), Adrienne, Nathan and Luke for whom the contents are designed as a guiding light into God's truth in love;

And, to my wife, Pam, whose undaunted love for me emulates and conveys to me God's marvelous love as described within these pages.

Table of Contents

Foreward

Paul's Epistle to the Romans is arguably the most important book ever written. It has certainly exerted an influence in the Christian Church that is second to none. And yet no other book has spurned such diverse interpretations. Competing interpretations of Paul's doctrine of justification by faith and his pronouncements on the destiny of Israel (in Chapters 9-11) are as contentious today as they were in the fourth or the sixteenth centuries. Both the significance of this Epistle and the difficulty of its interpretation have given rise to a vast literature on this book. With so much attention having been lavished upon this book, one is justified in wondering if there is need for yet another commentary.

This volume by Dr. R. Jeffrey Hiatt does fill a gap in treatments on Romans. Dr. Hiatt is a student of the Bible; but his training is primarily in historical theology. He thus brings the message of Romans into dialogue with the historical faith of the Church. Dr. Hiatt relates the meaning of Romans to the Church's theology not by imposing later theological issues upon the text of Romans, but by noting how Paul's thoughts derived from the text of Romans itself connects with and may be illumined by subsequent theological reflections of leaders in the community of faith.

But Dr. Hiatt's contribution goes beyond his deft conversation between Paul's thoughts and the theological tradition of the Church. Dr. Hiatt is a master in making the insights of NT scholars-insights that are typically offered in technical and highly arcane fashion understandable to the average person in the pew. Dr. Hiatt has immersed himself in the text of Romans and in the scholarly literature, and he draws from that rich reservoir to talk with us about Romans. It's almost as if he is conversing with us in our homes; one can almost smell the coffee and see the kitchen table.

Finally, Dr. Hiatt succeeds in connecting all the various strands in Paul's complex thought in this Epistle around Paul's missional aim of making Christ known to the world, and specifically at this point to Spain, and around the theological emphasis on the faithfulness of God. Dr. Hiatt skillfully shows as he moves from passage to passage, how all the sub-themes develop that major theological theme and thus fulfill Paul's ministerial aim. Dr. Hiatt constantly reminds readers of the larger picture, and shows how each passage relates to the broad program of the entire book.

This is a little book. But the smallness of its physical size belies its great helpfulness.

Dr. David R. Bauer
Asbury Theological Seminary
Dean of the School of Biblical Interpretation
Ralph Waldo Beeson Professor of Inductive Biblical Studies

Words from the Author

This work is intended to be an introduction for students and lay persons interested in a scholarly informed, but easily accessible, biblical study for personal or small group Christian formation. For technical scholarly arguments debating the variants, intricacies of nuanced interpretation, conclusions and decisions regarding the selection of each of the elements and its details, refer to the sources cited and their bibliographies.

Biblical translations are my own interpretation of scripture following the Nestle's Greek text and consulting with the NRSV, NASB, and NIV versions of the Bible.

Acknowledgments

I would like to thank my friend and esteemed colleague of eight years, Dr. Terry Swan, Dean of the Chapel and Religion Department Chair at Lindsey Wilson College, who asked me to contribute a chapter in a book project to introduce the New Testament to young college students who have little or no biblical exposure. This volume is the result of an expanded version of that project.

I express gratitude to Dr. Robert Danielson for his many hours of editing and eliminating my stylistic infelicities to make it smoother and more readable, and to his assistant, Faith Parry, who made corrections, and chased down details to finalize the process for publication.

Also, I appreciate my loving wife, Pam Hiatt, my partner in ministry for over 25 years, who read the manuscript, made suggestions and corrections to each of the many versions, and supported me through the long hours of its production.

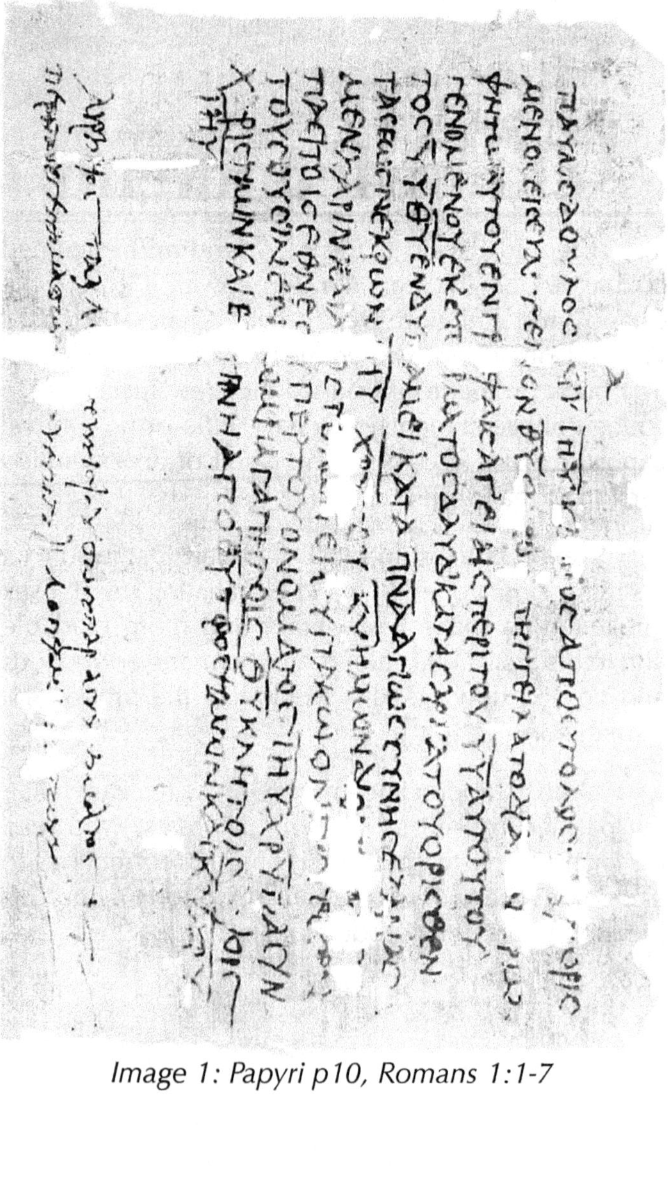

Image 1: Papyri p10, Romans 1:1-7

Introduction to Romans: Background

Context

In the first century AD, Rome was the ethnically diverse center of the Empire, with a population of about one million people in less than ten square miles.[1] The Jewish population, descended from the second century BC diaspora, was estimated at 40,000 to 50,000 within the city. In AD 64, after a large fire in Rome, Emperor Nero expelled the Jews. This also resulted in the first major persecution of the Church.

The city of Rome was predominately populated by Gentiles, so it is believed that the church was comprised of some Jewish, but mostly Gentile believers (cf. Romans 1:6, Romans 7:1). Paul addressed issues concerning both groups in this missionary correspondence.[2]

Image 2: Paul Writing His Epistles, painting probably by Valentin de Boulogne, 17th century.

Author and Recipients

Paul sent this letter to the Christians residing in the city of Rome (Romans 1:7, Romans 1:15).[3] While it is unclear how the churches in Rome originated, it is certain that Paul did not found the church there. The best explanation is that the Romans who were present at Pentecost (Acts 2:10-11) eventually made their way back to Rome and started a church in one of the synagogues on their own. "All roads lead to Rome" was the popular saying that demonstrated the city's importance and accessibility. It should not be surprising that there were already established churches there long before Paul's arrival. People who may have heard the gospel in Asia, Greece, or elsewhere could have traveled to Rome, also, adding to their growing numbers.

Place, and Date of Composition

In Romans 16:21-23, Paul named and extended greetings from Timothy, Lucius, Jason and Sosipater, Gaius,[4] Erastus, Quartus, Tertius (Paul's amanuensis) and himself to several people, including slaves and nobles, men and women, and Jews and Gentiles (cf. 16:3-15).[5] Recognizing Phoebe and Erastus as two prominent people from Corinth associated with this letter help us to identify this as the place of composition.[6]

Although Paul met some of the Roman Christians personally during their excursions from Rome, he did not know most of them, and they did not know him except by reputation. Therefore, Paul needed a more substantial introduction to the Church. One notable couple mentioned is Prisca[7] and Aquila. Both Aquila and Prisca were in Rome until about AD 49[8] when Claudius expelled all the Jews from the city (Acts 18:2). Paul met the couple when he came to Corinth (ca. AD 51). They did further ministry in Ephesus (Acts 18:19) around AD 53. From there they returned to Rome after the expulsion order lapsed. Prisca and Aquila were not likely the first ones to bring the gospel to Rome, either. Churches were already established, but as it is noted, Paul greeted the church that met in their house, too (Romans 16:5).[9] Thus, the Roman letter was likely composed after their return to Rome and probably was written during late AD 56 or early 57 from Corinth.[10]

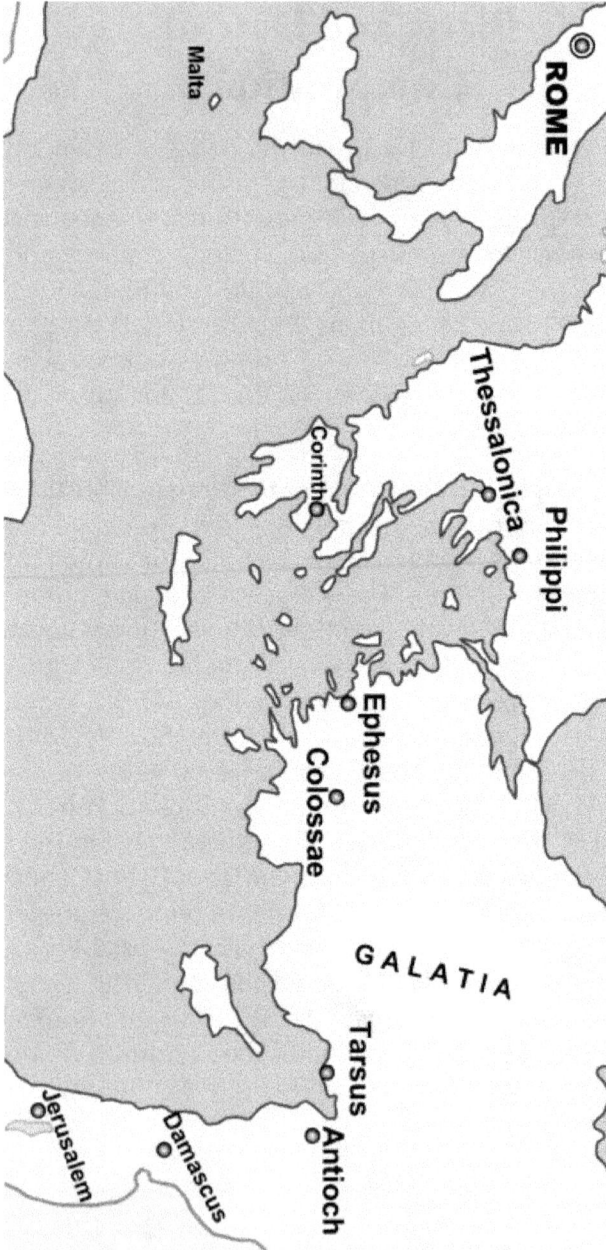

Image 3: Geographic map of Europe during Paul of Tarsus' times.

Overview of Themes, Significance, and Occasion of Composition

There is some debate about exactly where Paul's emphasis is in the material in Romans. What is clear is that there are dominant sub-themes, like movements in a symphony, in this missionary letter. In general, there had been a growing division between Gentile and Jewish Christians, and Paul wanted to reconcile this breach. These relationship concerns were a dominant feature in this writing.[11] Since salvation by grace through faith hinges on God's faithfulness, Paul dealt at length with what that means for "the Jew first, and also the Greek" (meaning Gentile, or non-Jew). The question is, "If God is not faithful to His promises to the Jews, how can the Gentiles trust him?" It is essentially the same question that the serpent raised in Genesis to Eve. Her doubt over the trustworthiness of God resulted in her lack of faith, lack of trust, and finally disobedience by both Eve and Adam. Paul's case presented in Romans was an attempt to explain that defection and highlight what God has done to heal, reconcile, and remedy that situation (cf. Romans 1-12).

One of the movements in the letter hints that there may have been divisions among the various congregations in Rome. These "house churches," or Christian fellowships, apparently needed to hear the gospel of impartial divine righteousness revealed in Christ. It is possible that each group's ethnocentric elements were dividing them from one another, as was the case elsewhere (cf. Galatians). Paul argued that Christ overturned the hierarchical honor system that divided and dominated the Mediterranean world. Jews and Gentiles were actually on the same footing before God—no exceptions! Paul wanted the house churches in the city to be an united family. Not only should this be a core characteristic of the "seamless robe of Christ." Paul desired united support for the next phase of carrying the gospel westward to the outer reaches of the empire.

The Roman Church's support of the mission to Spain (Romans 15:28) as proposed by the apostle, was crucial, and this may be the unifying thread of the letter.[12] Spain was a logistical problem, including various language groups other than Greek and Hebrew. Paul would need Roman support, possibly even translators. Paul also articulated exactly what he meant by the gospel of Christ. They must understand that what he was preaching was the same gospel proclaimed by the other apostles: the teachings and traditions of Jesus. Paul depended on the Holy Spirit for power to overcome evil and the ability to spread the gospel through a united Church. He desired that type of unit for the Roman Christians. It is likely, then, that Phoebe was sent to Rome with this letter to help to facilitate this important mission.[13]

Another sub-theme in the letter is to stimulate unity among all the believers. One way to accomplish this goal, was to collect money to send back to the persecuted Jerusalem church for their financial support. All of these issues are interrelated at a fundamental level. The collection also represented an acceptance of the legitimacy of the Gentile church by the Jewish church, as equal members of the Universal Church as constituted in Jesus Christ.

It is important to see Romans as a missionary letter in light of Paul's travels as an ambassador of the gospel to people and places who had not been exposed to the story of Christ, especially those that were situated along strategic travel routes. Paul had preached in Jerusalem, Judea and the surrounding area, and now was heading out to the "uttermost parts." In order to reach those places, it would take the united work of the church under the direction of the Holy Spirit.

Romans, with its prime feature of articulating the gospel according to Paul, is a fusion of at least three first-century letter types: the ambassadorial letter,[14] the hortatory letter, and the philosophical diatribe.[15] Romans is a situational letter that aims to persuade a united community of Roman house churches to pray for the "Jerusalem collection" and to help with Paul's projected mission to Spain.[16] The melody line of this "symphony" for Paul was "to make Christ known" (Romans 1:3-4; 3:21-26; 5:12-21; chapters 5-8).[17] Since Christ is the shared center-point of their lives as Christians, Paul's ideas and arguments keyed off of this base as a work of Christian rhetoric that aimed to persuade. "Paul knew Greek and Roman philosophy and worldviews, but he also knew how to correct them [with biblical exegetical precision]. This is one of the big things Romans accomplishes."[18] Thus, Romans is a summary of the gospel Paul preached and the practical implications for living and maturing in Christ.

Structure of Romans

The structure of Romans includes customary elements similar to other letters from first century Palestine. Paul provided, the introduction (1:1-15) with a thesis statement (1:16-17), the main body (1:18-15:13), and a conclusion (15:14-16:24) with the final doxology (16:25-27) to round out and conclude the letter.[19] The thrust of the main body provides an emphasis on his understanding of the gospel of Christ, and his apostolic/pastoral admonition concerning the unity of the believers. So, 1:18-4:25 focuses on the impartial righteousness of God that overturns all claims of ethno-superiority. Romans 5:1-8:39 emphasizes the Christ that replaces the quest for status through conformity to the Law. In Romans 9:1-11:36, Paul focuses on the triumph of God's righteousness in the gospel's mission to Israel and the Gentiles. Romans 12:1-15:13 centers on the personal and collective fruits of unity in the gospel. While 15:14-33 reveals Paul's mission and travel plans with an eye on global transformation. In 16:1-23, Paul commends Phoebe and gives personal greetings. He closes with a doxology in 16:25-27.

themselues, they departed, after that Paul had spoken one word, to wit, Well spake the holy Ghost by Esaias the Prophet vnto our fathers.

26 Saying, * Go vnto this people, and say, By hearing ye shall heare, and shall not vnderstand, and seing yee shall see, and not perceiue.

27 For the heart of this people is waxed fatte, and their eares are dull of hearing, and with their eyes haue they winked, least they should see with their eyes, and heare with their eares, and vnderstande with their hearts, and should returne that I might heale them.

28 Be it knowen therefore vnto you, that this saluation of God is sent to the Gentiles, and they shall heare it.

29 And when he had sayd these things, the Iewes departed, and had great reasoning among themselues.

30 And Paul remained two yeeres full in an house hired for himselfe, and receiued all that came in vnto him,

31 Preaching the kingdome of God, and teaching those things, which concerne the Lorde Iesus Christ, with all boldnesse of speech, without let.

*Isa.6.9. mat.13.14 mer.4.12.
Luke 8.10. ioh.12.40.rom.11.8.*
k Hereby the hearts of the infidels ought to be mollified, and the wicklings confirmed, that they be not offended by the stubbornes of the wicked.

1 The Word of God healeth when the vertue of the Spirit is ioyned with it: and it is preached generally, that all men might be inexcusable.

The Epistle of the Apostle Paul
to the Romanes.

THE ARGVMENT.

THe great mercie of God is declared toward man in Christ Iesus, whose righteousnesse is made ours through faith. For when man by reason of his own corruption could not fulfil the Law, yea, committed most abominably, both against the law of God, and nature, the infinite bountie of God, mindfull of his promise made to his seruant Abraham, the father of all beleeuers, ordeined that mans saluation should only stand in the perfect obedience of his Sonne Iesus Christ : so that not only the circumcised Iewes, but also the vncircumcised Gentiles should be saued by faith in him : euen as Abraham before he was circumcised, was counted iust only through faith, & yet afterward receiued circumcision, as a seale or badge of the same righteousnesse by faith. And to the intent that none should thinke that the couenant which God made to him, and his posteritie was not performed: either because the Iewes receiued not Christ, (which was the blessed seede) or els beleeued not that he was the true redeemer, because he did not only, or at least more notably preserue the Iewes : the examples of Ismael and Esau declare, that all are not Abrahams posteritie, which come of Abraham according to the flesh: but also the very strangers and Gentiles grafted in by faith, are made heires of the promise. The cause wherof is the only will of God, forasmuch as of his free mercy he electeth some to be saued, and of his iust iudgement reiecteth others to be damned, as appeareth by the testimonies of the Scriptures. Yet to the intent that the Iewes should not be too much beaten downe, nor the Gentiles too much puffed vp, the example of Elias prooueth, that God hath yet his elect euen of the naturall posteritie of Abraham, though it appeareth not so to mans eye: and for that preferment that the Gentiles haue, it proceedeth of the liberal mercy of God, which he at length will stretch toward the Iewes againe, and so gather the whole Israel (which is his Church) of them both. This ground-works of faith & doctrine laied, instructions of Christian maners follow: reaching euery man to walke in soundnesse of conscience in his vocation, with all patience and humblenesse, reuerencing and obeying the magistrate, exercising charity, putting off the old man, and putting on Christ, bearing with the weake, and louing one another according to Christs example. Finally, S. Paul after his commendations to the brethren, exhorteth them to vnitie, and to flee false preachers and flatterers, and so concludeth with a prayer.

CHAP. I.

1 *Paul sheweth by whom, and to what purpose he is called.* 13 *His ready will.* 16 *What the Gospell is.* 20 *The vse of creatures, and wherefore they were made.* 21.24 *The ingratitude, peruersitie and punishment of all mankind.*

1 Or, minister.
a Through Gods mercie, and also appointed by commandement to this Apostleship.
b Or chosen by the eternal counsell of God, or by the declaration of the same counsell.

PAVL a seruant of Iesus Christ, * called to be an Apostle, b * put a part to preach the Gospel of God,

2 (Which he had promised afore by his *Prophets in the * holy Scriptures)

3 Concerning his Sonne Iesus Christ our Lord (which was made of the * seede of Dauid according to the flesh,

4 And declared mightily to be the Sonne of God, touching the Spirit of e sanctification by the resurrection from the dead)

5 By whom wee haue receiued f grace and Apostleship (that obedience might bee giuen vnto the faith) in his Name among all the Gentiles,

6 Among whom ye be also the c called of Iesus Christ,

7 To all you that be at Rome beloued of God, called to be Saincts: * b Grace be with you, and peace from God our Father, and from the Lord Iesus Christ.

8 First I thanke my God through IBSVS Christ for you all, because your faith is published throughout the whole world.

9 For God is my witnes (whom I serue in my * spirit in the * Gospel of his Sonne) that without ceasing I make mention of you

Acts 23.1. Deut.18.15. after 3.22. c The Scriptures onely set foorth the great benefite of God promised and performed to the world in Iesus Christ, d Meaning of the posteritie, and of the flesh of the virgine Marie,

1.Cor.1.2. gal.1.3. 2.tim.1.2. h The free mercie of God, and prosperous successe in all things. i That is, through all Christian Churches, k Earnestly, and from the heart. l In preaching the Sonne of God, that is reconciliation and peace through Christ.

c By the Spirit he declareth that Christ is God, whose power did so sanctifie his humanitie, that it could not feele corruption, nor yet remaine in death.
f Which was that most liberall benefite to preach the vnsearchable riches of Christ.
g That is, by the mercy of God in Iesus Christ.

10 Alwayes

Romans

Image 5: The Greek text of Romans 1:1-1:28
from the Codex Vaticanus B (pg. 1445).

Outline of Romans

I. Introduction: Paul's Preview of the Gospel (1:1-17)

II. God's Righteousness Explained (1:18-11:36)
 A. God's Righteousness: A Universal
   Need (1:18-3:20)
 B. God's Righteousness: Justification
   and Sanctification (3:21-8:39)
    1. Justification: The Rectifying of Life (3:21-4:25)
    2. Sanctification: The Transforming
      of Life (5:1-8:39)
 C. God's Righteousness: Obtained
   by Faith (9:1-11:36)

III. Christian Formation (12:1-15:13)
 A. Love Expressed as Worship (12:1-2)
 B. Love Expressed in Unity
   (12:3-13)
 C. Love Expressed in the Neighborhood
   (12:14-15:13)

IV. Mission Critical Plans and People (15:14-16:23)
 A. Mission Critical Plans (15:14-33)
 B. Mission Critical People (16:1-27)

V. Doxological Conclusion (16:25-27)

I. Introduction: Paul's Preview of the Gospel (1:1-17)

Paul, a Jew, set out at the beginning of this letter to proclaim boldly that the center of his life is Jesus. God has commissioned him to bear the gospel of Christ to as many people as who would hear him, but especially to non-Jews, the Gentiles (1:1-6). He was a missionary. Paul put forth a clear account of his missionary life led by the gospel of Christ. He was not writing his memoirs, but, he was highlighting the saga of the gospel.

1 Paul, a slave of Christ Jesus, called to be an apostle, set apart for the gospel of God ²which was promised beforehand through his prophets in the Holy Scriptures, ³concerning his Son, who came to be born as a physical descendant of David, ⁴who was appointed the Son

of God in power through the Spirit of holiness by his resurrection from the dead, Jesus Christ our Lord, [5]through whom we received grace and apostleship unto the obedience that comes from faith to call all the Gentiles for his name's sake, [6]among whom you also are called of Jesus Christ. [7]To all those in Rome, beloved by God, called saints. Grace and peace to you from God our Father and from the Lord Jesus Christ.

[8]First of all, I thank my God through Jesus Christ for all of you, because your faith is being proclaimed all over the world. [9]For God is my witness, whom I serve in my spirit in the gospel of his Son, how ceaselessly I remember you [10]always in my prayers; praying if somehow that now at last by God's will a good route may be opened for me to come to you. [11]I long to see you so that I may share some spiritual gift to strengthen you. [12]That is, that you and I be mutually encouraged by each other's faith.

[13]I do not want you to be ignorant, brothers and sisters how often I wanted to come to you (and was prevented from doing so until now) in order that I might have some fruit among you, just as I have had among the other Gentiles. [14]I am indebted to both to Greeks and non-Greeks, both to the wise and the foolish. [15]Hence, that is why I eagerly desire to preach the gospel also to you who are in Rome.

There is no more respectful way to greet someone than to pray that God will give them His favor and a full life of God's best material and non-material blessings (1:7). Just like the Thessalonians, the faith of the Christian in Rome was being talked about positively in many places around the region (1:8).

Paul had not been to Rome to see these Christians before, and he did not start any of the churches there. However, he had been continually praying for them, and was eager to meet them in person. He believed that not only could he be a blessing to them, but that they could be a blessing to him, and a solid part of his ministry to others who had never heard the gospel (1:9-15).

The heart of the letter is anchored in these few words:

>[16]For I am not ashamed of the gospel, for it is God's power leading to salvation to everyone who has faith, to the Jew first and also to the Greek. [17]For in the gospel the righteousness of God is revealed from faith to faith, just as it is written, "the one who is righteous-by-faith will live."

Paul established the direction that he planned to take in the rest of the letter: he would elaborate on the gospel and its implications. This would include discussing Jews and Gentiles, broadly speaking, and more narrowly, their relationships one to another as Christian believers. Since the gospel is not to be confined to any single location, Paul also indicated the traveling nature of the gospel.

Paul was eager to preach the gospel, because it is the effective power of God to save people now and in the future from the destructive power of sin. Salvation is available to all, irrespective of race, on the basis of faith and trust. The Gospel reveals God's Way, the way of righteousness, which is open to humanity based on trust in Him: "The one who is righteous-by-faith shall live."

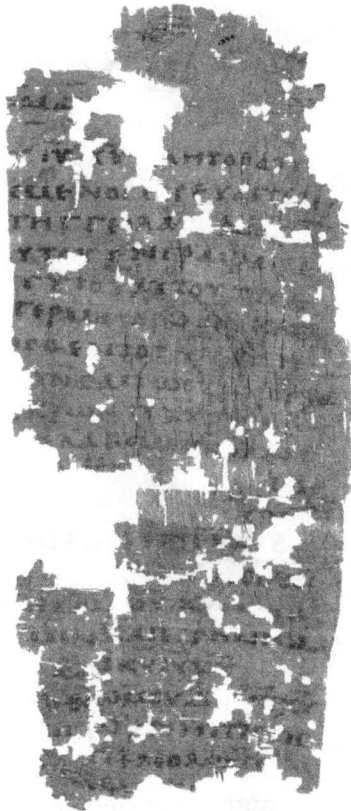

Image 6: Papyri p26, Romans 1:1-10

II. God's Righteousness Explained (1:18-11:36)

[20]In order to explain God's righteousness, Paul began with the bad news. We are not righteous. In fact, no one is. It is a universal predicament.[21] Even more disconcerting is that Paul elaborated the case for our destruction, emphasizing sin, wrath, and judgment. There is no escape on our own.

A. God's Righteousness: A Universal Need (1:18-3:20)

◇◇◇

[18]For the wrath of God is being revealed from heaven against every form of godlessness and human injustice, who suppress the truth by their unrighteousness, [19]for what may be known about God is

evident among them, because God has made himself plain to them. [20]For since the creation of the world God's invisible nature—his eternal power and deity—have been seen, being understood from what has been made, so that they are without excuse.

[21]Because, although they knew God, they neither glorified him nor gave thanks to him as God, but became empty-headed in their reasonings, and their foolish hearts were darkened. [22]Claiming to be wise, they became foolish [23]and exchanged the glory of the immortal God for the likeness of images made to look like mortal human beings, birds, animals, and reptiles.

[24]Therefore God handed them over in the desires of their hearts to impurity for the degrading of their bodies with one another. [25]They exchanged the truth of God for a lie, and worshiped and served the creature rather than the Creator, who is praised forever. Amen.

[26]Because of this, God handed them over to dishonorable lusts, for women exchanged natural sexual relations for ones against nature, [27]and similarly, the men, leaving natural relations with women, and burned in their lust for one another, men with other men, doing that which is shameful and receiving in themselves the inevitable penalty for their perversion. [28]Just as they did not see fit to retain the

knowledge of God, so God gave them up to a discredited mind, so that they do what is not right, [29]being filled with every kind of unrighteousness (evil, greed malice, full of envy, murder, strife, deceit, maligners, gossips, [30]slanderers, God-haters, insolent, arrogant, boastful, inventers of evil, disobedient to parents, [31]without discernment, without fidelity, without natural affection, without mercy), [32]who, know God's righteous pronouncements, that those who do such things deserve death, not only continue to do these things, but even approve of those who practice them.

In 1:18-32, Paul mainly targeted the gentile world.[22] Paul could make this point because of our "ungodliness," that is, we worship something else besides God (idolatry), and our "wickedness" (sexual sins especially), but also because we suppress the truth (1:18).[23] He took a hardline stand, because God's invisible power and divine nature can still be discerned through creation, no mater how dim, and it leaves no room for excuses (1:19-20). That is to say, it is not ignorance that God condemns *per se*, but *intentional* ignorance, and an outright refusal to acknowledge God as God (1:21).

The consequences for people rejecting God are severe. God "gives them up" to the object of their narcissism and affection--themselves (1:22-25)! Each one has strayed by turning to his own foolish way (Isaiah 53). Turning away from God, means that we turn in upon ourselves. Self-centered living churns up all kinds of destructive behaviors and debauched desires (1:24-32). Losing our ability to discern God's will (1:28), God's wrath becomes evident in that God has left us to be alone with our illicit, illegitimate, and lustful choices.

In the list of vices that Paul cites, he conveyed what is the common experience of people everywhere. This universal plague of sin is destroying human beings as they exchange godliness for their unnatural desires for degrading behavior, active mischief against the property of others, and willful malicious acts of injustice to satisfy their own greedy cravings.[24]

Thus far, in 1:18-32, Paul illuminated "the nature and progress of sin: (1) Ingratitude, 21; (2) Idolatry, 25; and (3) Moral degradation, 26-32."[25] Paul gave a terrible picture of what happens when people or nations intentionally banish God from their ways. "Disaster and degeneracy [go] hand in hand."[26]

The need for justification is amply shown by the facts of the human condition. These show everywhere the outworking of the wrath of God in condemning human wickedness. For although God has revealed himself through the created order, humans have suppressed that knowledge, with hideous results. Refusing to acknowledge God as God, humans sank to the lever of worshiping the beasts. Since humans thus chose sin, God let them have it to make plain the depth of their squalor: dishonesty, idolatry, sexual and other forms of perversion which they not only committed, but rejoiced in.

In 2:1-3:8, Paul was mainly concerned with the Jews.[27] A main thrust is to demonstrate the impartiality of God. No one has advance standing on ethnic privilege, or by good works. The attitudes and vices listed or alluded to in the previous section is also brought to bear on the person who stands ready to condemn[28] others. The problem is the accuser stands guilty of the "same things." They cannot be off the hook since they *should* know better because of the specific instructions of the Lord given to them in the Torah (Law). The Jews believed that they could "get away with" the same vices that they condemned in the Gentiles because of their special relationship to God. This type of thinking is hypocrisy and Paul proceeds to dismantle the assumed special privilege of not being subject to the wrath of God, which was such a prevalent understanding among his Jewish contemporaries. Paul made it clear that presumption on God's forbearance is not the same thing as faith, and presuming on God's mercy, instead of repenting, is actually disdain for God, and *that* is deadly.

◇◇

2 Therefore, you have no excuse, each one of you who is judging someone else, for in whatever matter you judge another, you are condemning yourself, because you who are judging do the same things. [2]But we know that God's judgment against those who do such things is according to truth. [3]So when you, oh human being, judge others and yet do the same things, do you think you will escape God's judgment? [4]Or do you make light of the riches of his kindness, forbearance and patience, being unaware that God's kindness is intended to lead you to repentance?

⁵But because of your hard and your unrepentant heart, you are storing up wrath against yourself on the day of God's wrath, and the revelation of his righteous judgment, ⁶when God "will repay each person according to what they have done." ⁷On the one hand, to those who by persistence in doing good seek glory, honor and immortality, he will give eternal life. ⁸But, on the other hand, for those who are selfish and who reject the truth and follow unrighteousness, wrath and anger, ⁹there will be trouble and distress on every human being who does evil: first to the Jew, then for the Greek; ¹⁰but there is glory, honor and peace for everyone who does good: first to the Jew, then for the Greek. ¹¹For God does not show partiality.

Paul wanted to set the record straight! The Jewish special relationship lay in being the chosen group of people through whom the promise of God the Father would come to the world, namely, the Messiah, Jesus Christ, and the subsequent out pouring of the Holy Spirit in fulfilling previous prophetic promises (2:16). What it did not entail was for anyone to be able to plunge headlong into a sinful disregard of God and lack of holy love for their neighbor. This disposition and behavior would not be tolerated by God from anyone, Jew or Gentile. Thus, they stood under the same condemnation for the same reasons. Even if it was on the basis of different types of revelation, it was still the same standard of holy love that was used to measure sinfulness (2:1-11).[29]

If someone repents, then God's wrath is averted (2:4-5). If they persist in stubbornness and going their own way, then evil, judgment, and wrath, will be their earned allotment and finally, they will perish (2:6-12). He spelled out that it is not the hearers of the Law (commands, instructions, or requirements) who are "declared to be right," or set right (justified), but those who *act on these commands in faith* and truth. If we miss this point, then we disregard God's enabling power and real transformation of the heart that produces a "Christian" lifestyle noted by God's "real change in the heart" (or sanctifying work) in the believer (cf. 12:1-2ff)! However, at this stage of Paul's case, he also points out that "doing" (or being obedient to) what God commands is actually important, as well (2:12-16). Nonetheless, "doing" is not the *basis* of our righteousness, but it should be a fruit of it.

[12]For whoever sins outside the Law will also perish outside the Law, and all who sin under the Law will be judged by the Law. [13]For it is not those who hear the Law who are righteous in God's sight, but it is those who obey the Law who will be declared righteous. [14]For, when Gentiles, who do not have the Law, do by nature things required by the Law, they are a law for themselves, even though they do not have the Law. [15]They show that the works of the Law are written on their hearts, their

consciences bearing witness, and their
thoughts sometimes accusing and other
times defending them, [16]on the day when
God judges human secrets through Jesus
Christ, according to my gospel.

The point that Paul was driving home is the
universal condemnation that is the result of the
reign of sin. He was setting up the discussion of the
basis for justification. Justification is being put in a
right relationship to/with God, on the basis of *grace
through faith in Christ.* The outcome is that we are
able to keep the commands of the gospel because of
the enabling power of the Holy Spirit at work within
us.

If anyone, Jew or Gentile, is inclined to join in
the chorus of condemnation, please reconsider. In
condemning others the condemner will only find
condemnation because of doing the very same
things. The patience of God should not be mistaken
for indifference; its purpose is rather to give time for
repentance. To refuse to repent is to store up God's
anger for the "day of wrath." On that day, goodness
and sin will receive their due reward without partiality
to either Jew or Gentile. The basis of judgment will be
knowledge and the corresponding obedience to this
kowledge. In the case of the Jews, this knowledge
will be the Law (2:12); in the case of the Gentiles, it is
the moral deliverance of their conscience (2:15).

[17]Now if you call yourself a Jew, rely on the
Law, and boast in God, [18] know his will
and approve of what is best because you

are instructed by the Law, [19]are convinced that you are a guide to the blind, a light to those who are in darkness, [20]an instructor of the foolish, a teacher of the immature, because you have the embodiment of knowledge and truth in the Law — [21]so, then, you who teach others, do you not teach yourself? Do you who preach against stealing, steal? [22]Do you who say not to commit adultery, commit adultery? Do you who abhor idols, rob temples? [23]Do you who boast in the Law, dishonor God by breaking the Law? [24]As it is written: "God's name is blasphemed among the nations because of you."

[25]Circumcision has value if you do the Law, but if you break the Law, you have become uncircumcised. [26]So then, if those who are not circumcised keep the Law's requirements, will they not be reckoned as circumcision? [27]The one who is not circumcised physically and yet obeys the Law will condemn you, even though you have the written code and circumcision, break the Law. [28]A Jew is not who is one only outwardly, nor is it outward circumcision in the flesh that is the circumcision, [29]but a person is a Jew who is one inwardly, and who has circumcision of the heart, in the spirit, not by the letter, whose praise is not from other people, but from God.

In 2:17-29, Paul acknowledged the purpose of the Jews who followed the teachings of Moses to be a light to the nations, a guide to the blind, and an instructor to the foolish. God's revelation was true regardless of how they practiced it. Even if they were not faithful, God was. Even if they acted unjustly, God would act with justice.

Now, Paul makes a turn in his argument. He has already implied that written instructions are limited, holy as they are. They are not complete in themselves. Outward conformity does not make one a faithful follower of God, but the inner conformity that results in living by the principles that God teaches. This is not done by conformity to a code, but in the human spirit by the transforming of the Holy Spirit. It is not by physical circumcision of the body, but by "circumcision" of the heart. In the human spirit, the Holy Spirit "can operate inwardly in a way that a written code cannot."[30]

If being a Jew brought any privilege of religious enlightenment, it also brought the corresponding responsibility, namely of living in conformity with that light. This was where the Jewish people had failed, and that failure caused the name of God to stink among the Gentiles (2:17-24). Failure of this magnitude had another severe consequence. It disqualified one from being a real Jew by nullifying the effect of circumcision. Because "circumcision" does not consist of an outward alteration of the flesh but an inner renewal of the heart. This means, tragically, that a Jew-in-the-flesh can cease to be a Jew-in-the-heart. It also means that a Gentile-in-the-flesh can become a Jew-in-the-heart. Paul unveiled the idea that a good Gentile was actually better than a bad Jew (2:25-29).

3 What, then, is the advantage in being a Jew, or what benefit is there in circumcision? ²Much in every way. First of all, the Jews have been entrusted with the words of God. ³What if some were unfaithful? Will their unfaithfulness nullify God's faithfulness? ⁴Of course not! Let God be true, even if every human being is a liar. As it is written: "So that you may be vindicated when you speak and prevail when you are tried." ⁵But if our unrighteousness shows God's righteousness more clearly, what shall we say? That God is unrighteous in bringing his wrath on us? (I am using human logic.) ⁶Of course not! If that were so, how could God judge the world? ⁷And, "If the truth of God so increases his glory in my refusal of the truth, why am I still being condemned as a sinner?" ⁸Why not conclude—just as some slanderously claim that we say—"Do evil that good may come"? Their condemnation is deserved!

In 3:1-8, the rhetorical question was posed that if all are under the judgment of God as a result of universal sin, then what advantage does the Jew have, being the elect, chosen ones of God? Paul was decisive in pointing out that this advantage was having the "oracles of God," a "divine message,"³¹ the Scriptures (3:2). Having the truth explained about God's judgment and the plan of salvation is a great advantage, because it clearly explains the character and disposition of God toward Creation, in general, and toward humans in particular. The Jews were entrusted with this message to be given to the whole world. At one level, they were stewards of God's grace. The people of God were to be like the boy's lunch of bread and fish which Jesus blessed, so that when it was given away, it multiplied and fed thousands. God's people were not to be like hoarded manna that rotted and bred maggots!

God was faithful to His mission, even though Israel had not kept her part of the relationship: she failed in delivering the message of God to her neighbors and the surrounding nations had become distrustful of God. God is not deterred by human failure. Paul will get around to the point that Jesus the Messiah is delivering the message as faithfully intended by God.[32] What is needed is reconciliation, the "restoration of a positive relationship to God" (in righteousness).[33]

The Jewish objection to Paul's argument was because it made them no better than the Gentiles. Paul was emphatic that they were not better, but they did have advantages. The first advantage was that they were custodians of the Scriptures (3:1-2). What about their faithlessness? Human faithlessness does not and cannot nullify God's faithfulness (3:3-4). If human faithlessness highlights God's faithfulness, how can He fairly judge those who are faithless? Paul answered the objection with a question whose answer is obvious: How could God be the righteous Judge of the Earth without punishing sin (3:5-6)? But, if God's glory is emphasized because of my sin, then why am I condemned? Why can't I do evil so that good may come? Such logic is self-condemning (3:7-8)!

⁹What, then, shall we conclude? Are we superior? Not at all! For we have already made the accusation that all people, Jews and Gentiles alike, are all under the power of sin. ¹⁰As it is written: "There are none righteous, not even one; ¹¹no one understands; none are seeking out God. ¹²All have turned away, they have together gone wrong; no one does good, not even one."³⁴ ¹³"Their throats are open graves; their tongues deceive." "The poison of snakes is on their lips." ¹⁴"Their mouth is full of curses and bitterness." ¹⁵"Their feet are swift to shed blood. ¹⁶Ruin and misery march their path, ¹⁷and the way of peace they do not know." ¹⁸"There is no fear of God before their eyes."

¹⁹Now we know that whatever the Law says, it speaks to those who are under the Law, in order that every mouth may be stopped and the whole world be held guilty before God. ²⁰Therefore no one will be declared righteous before God by the works of the Law; rather, through the Law we become conscious of sin.

Then, in 3:9-20, Paul summarized the case he had made up to this point, namely, that Gentiles and Jews alike are indicted "under the power of sin" (9b-18).³⁵ It is in fact, the Law (the Torah) that holds the Jew, in particular, accountable for sin. It defines what sin is, and makes it known for what it is, revealing guilt before God. So everyone is silenced before God. No

R. JEFFREY HIATT | 33

one can practice rebellion against God and get away with it. No one. Period!

At the Divine Judgment Seat, the verdict is that all are guilty and condemned; none are able to escape by anything they can do based on themselves. While the Law reveals human sinfulness, it cannot do anything to cure it (3:19-20). The picture could not be any worse from this point of view. God has won the case against us, and we have lost it all. Is there any hope? If this were the final word, we would all despair, and we would be weeping, wailing, and gnashing our teeth!

B. God's Righteousness: Justification and Sanctification (3:21-8:39)

The question is, "How can a person be right with God?" How can a person who is afraid of God have peace with God? The Law is designed to show the utter wickedness of sin! It results in bringing the person who hopes to achieve personal righteousness on their own to despair. It is impossible. If we were innocent, we could be acquitted. But, since we are guilty, what then? The emphasis in the previous section was on what humans were doing and the dismal results of these actions. The death penalty is on the table. Paul has laid out the case, and the end for the guilty is a fair execution.

Here is where the plot takes a twist. The verdict is clear: "Guilty on all charges of sin." The punishment that fits the crime is death (3:23a). But, God has not yet pronounced the sentence. Humans have failed, but God has succeeded. The Good News has arrived. Paul is careful to describe "the new era that has tiptoed nearer" and finally is now dawning.[36]

1. Justification: The Rectifying of Life (3:21-4:25)

◇◇◇

[21]But now apart from the Law the righteousness of God has been made clear, which the Law and the Prophets attest, [22]the righteousness of God through the faithfulness of Jesus Christ to all who believe. There is no distinction between Jew and Gentile, [23]for all have sinned and lack the glory of God, [24]being righteous freely by his grace through the redemption that came by Christ Jesus. [25]God set forth Christ as a sacrifice of atonement through faith in his blood, for a demonstration of his righteousness, because in his forbearance he had passed over the sins committed beforehand [26]to demonstrate his righteousness at the present time, so as to be righteous and the one who sets right those who have faith in Jesus.

[27]Where, then, is boasting? It is precluded. Through what law? Of works? No, through the law of faith. [28]For we reckon that a person is righteous by faith apart from the works of the Law. [29]Or is God

the God of Jews alone? Is he not also the God of Gentiles? Yes, of Gentiles too. [30]Since there is only one God, who sets right the circumcised by faith and the uncircumcised through the same faith. [31]Do we, then, nullify the Law through faith? Of course not! Rather, we confirm the Law.

◇◇◇

It is God's righteousness, i.e., His righteous character and His path for putting humanity in right relationship with Himself, "being set right, being set on the right moral course" that is being revealed now as was foreshadowed by the Law and the Prophets (3:21).[37] Paul now explains what he means by "his gospel." It is based on trust in Christ, and available to all who will trust. Since all have sinned without distinction, all may be saved by trust in Christ without distinction (3:22-24). God is the Giver of the grace that allows this salvation to occur (3:24b), but it is brought to us through the work of Christ. God puts forth Jesus to conquer sin which the Law could not do (3:24-25a). The twin objectives of this act of God are to vindicate God's righteous character and "to make people righteous in the present" (3:25b-26).[38] There is a stay of execution for those who trust Christ. God pardons the guilty through faith in Jesus Christ! Rejoice, and again I say, rejoice!

Paul now returns to the theme set out in 1:16-17, namely, how the power of the gospel plays out. God is doing a new thing. Paul set out to describe how the Law is fulfilled in Christ. It is not by works; it is by faith or trust in Jesus. What God has done in Christ both finishes the requirements of the old covenant and sets forth the new one. But in the new covenant there is still continuity, because even the old covenant was not based on works, but on faith or trust in God.[39] What is new about this covenant is that God has come in the flesh and "tabernacled among us." Just like He did in the wilderness in the tent of meeting, but now, God is visible, yet veiled, in the person of Jesus. "Veiled in flesh the God-head see; Hail the incarnate Deity," wrote Charles Wesley.

It is the same God, but with a new place of meeting available to all! The argument here could not be clearer. Paul wanted to highlight that under the old age, all were equally condemned because of the universality of sin (3:23). In contrast, all who believe in Christ are rescued. By Christ's work through his death, because "God was in Christ reconciling the world to himself" (2 Corinthians 5:19), God can justly turn away his wrath from those who trust Christ, and remove their human sin, making them righteous (3:25b-26). Although Paul used metaphorical language to describe God's work in salvation; "being set right" (a legal metaphor), redemption (a metaphor from slavery), and atonement (a sacrificial metaphor),[40] we need to listen to his main point. Ben Witherington III insightfully puts it this way,

> Paul...is describing real spiritual transactions that resulted from the historical death of Christ. God's wrath against sin was assuaged, humans were cleansed from their sin, (both propitiation and expiation being involved), they were set free from the bondage of sin (redemption), and they were set back in right relationship with God and with each other (atonement),

if only they will appropriate these benefits through faith.[41]

The consequences of Justification by faith work their way out in the lives of those who trust in Jesus in two ways: 1) Since people are justified not by deeds but by trust in what God has done for them, there is no room for bragging or boasting. Salvation is by faith, so there is nothing humanly to boast about (3:27-28). 2) If God justifies the Jews by faith—and he does—since there is only one God, He must also "set right" the Gentiles in the same way (by faith), putting both on the same footing (3:29-30). When Paul was accused of making null the Law by his gospel of faith, he countered on the grounds that it rather fulfills its deeper principles. A look at the story of Abraham reveals this truth (3:31).

◇◇◇

4 What then shall we say that Abraham, our forefather according to the flesh, obtained? [2]If, in fact, Abraham was set right by works, he had something to boast about—but not before God. [3]For what does Scripture say? "Abraham believed God, and it was reckoned[42] to him as righteousness." [4]Now for the one who works, wages are not credited as a gift but as what is due. [5]But, to the one who does not work but trusts God who justifies the ungodly, their faith is reckoned as righteousness. [6]David says the same thing when he speaks a blessing over the one to whom God reckons as righteousness apart from works: [7]"Blessed are those whose transgressions are forgiven, whose sins are covered. [8]Blessed is the one whose sin the Lord does not reckon against them."

[9]Therefore, is this blessing only for the circumcised or for the uncircumcised also? We have been saying that Abraham's faith was reckoned to him as righteousness. [10]How was it credited? Was it after he was circumcised, or when he was uncircumcised? It was not after, but before! [11]And he received circumcision as a sign, a seal of the righteousness of faith of those who are uncircumcised, so that, he is the father of all who believe but have not been circumcised, in order that righteousness might be reckoned to them. [12]And he is then also the father of the circumcised who not only are circumcised but who also follow in the footsteps of faith that our father Abraham had before he was circumcised.

[13]For the promise to Abraham or his offspring came not through the Law that they would be heirs of the world, but through the righteousness of faith, [14]for if those who depend on the Law are heirs, faith is invalidated and the promise is nullified. [15]The Law brings wrath. But where there is no law, neither is there transgression. [16]For this reason, the promise comes by faith, so that it may be by grace and may be confirmed to all Abraham's offspring, not only to those who are of the Law but also to those who have the faith of Abraham, who is the

father of us all. [17]Just as it is written: "I have appointed you as the father of many nations." The God in whom he believed is the God who gives life to the dead and calls into being things that were not,

[18]against all hope, Abraham with hope believed and so became the father of many nations, just as it had been said, "So shall your offspring be." [19]Without weakening in his faith, he faced the fact that his body was as good as dead, since he was about a hundred years old, and that Sarah's womb was also dead, [20]but he did not waver in unfaith regarding the promise of God, but was strengthened in his faith and gave glory to God, [21]being fully persuaded that God had power to do what he had promised. [22]Therefore, "it was reckoned to him for righteousness."

[23]The words "it was reckoned to him" were written not for him alone, [24]but also for us, to whom God will account righteousness, for those who believe in him who raised Jesus our Lord from the dead, [25]who was handed over to death for our transgressions and was raised to life for our being set right.

Abraham was made righteous on the basis of faith, not works, as Paul's detractors supposed (4:1-25). "Abraham believed [trusted] God and it was reckoned [accounted] to Him as righteousness," Paul declared in 4:3, interpreting Genesis 15:6. Paul was hammering home that we are saved by the grace of God through faith in Christ.[43] This is a *sine qua non* in Paul's argument. If Abraham is made righteous because of his Law-keeping, then he has something to boast about, because he has received his righteousness as payment for something he has done (4:2-8).[44]

Paul cut away any pretense of a works-based righteousness (4:5). He continued to put the foundation together for the inclusion of his ministry to the Gentiles as a legitimate expression of God's initiative (4:9-12) and intention all along. Abraham was a Gentile idolater before God called him. What changed? How did he become "a Jew" or become "righteous?" It was "through God's initiative in giving to him an unmerited *gift* [grace], and by his trusting and obedient acceptance of that gift."[45] Abraham's "being set right" and the attendant promise cannot be explained as coming through the Law. Faith and law belong to different worlds. The Law, because of our failure to keep it, brings wrath, not forgiveness, or pardon. This is the reason that the promise is conditioned upon faith. Only upon the basis of grace can the promise be secured for Jew and Gentile alike, which must be to be true, since Abraham is to be the father of many nations as Scripture declares (4:13-17).

Paul put this example forward as the pattern of the divine-human relationship. It always begins with God's gift, and is received via human trust.[46] Paul has invoked that blessing and the support of Abraham for his point, but he moved to another important example when he enlisted the support of a Psalm of King David, recalling the golden era of Jewish history, to strengthen and confirm his view as well. He demonstrated the link through Psalm 32:1-2 (Romans 4:7-8) that God forgives and does not "reckon" sin against the one who trusts in the Lord. Paul then makes the leap of faith to the current Christian position based on grace through faith.[47]

The quality of Abraham's faith fits his title. He trusted God as the One who gives life to the dead. Physically, the fulfillment of the promise of a child seemed impossible because of Abraham and Sarah's advanced years. This challenged his faith, but did not extinguish it, and God accounted his trust as righteousness (4:18-22). The principle of justification applies to Abraham and to everyone else who trusts in the God who raised Jesus from the dead to procure our pardon from sin (4:23-25).

In summary, Paul spent the fourth chapter of Romans adding precise elements to his case so that trust/faith has a prior position over the works themselves. Works flow from faith/trust, not visa versa. Paul concentrates and articulates most of his key themes in Romans through this section: righteousness by faith (4:9-12); God as a God of mercy; the priority of grace over Law (4:13-17); the anticipation of Christ in the Old Testament story of Israel (4:17b-22); and the significance of promise (4:18-22).[48] This secures the open door for other Gentiles to come to Christ based on trust in God through Christ over the Law (4:13-22). Paul's discussion through chapter four showed Abraham as the common ancestor of both Jews and Gentiles, but more than scions, they are heirs of the Spirit through faith. Even in the face of the impossible, Abraham trusted God. Since he trusted God, he stands in a right relationship to God.[49] God demonstrated that God is trustworthy. Paul also points to God's character of trustworthiness as a reason that God has always intended to include the Gentiles in the salvation mission.[50] There is no distinction between Jew and Gentile. First, both are under the power of sin (3:9), and second, both can only be justified (set right) by faith (3:28-30); salvation, then, is available to all people everywhere on the same basis of grace through faith.

This is part of Paul's design to heal the attitudes of both Christian Jews and Gentiles toward one another. Using this letter in preparation for his visit, Paul wanted to foster a deeper unity among the believers, as well as to put the theological issues on the table, before he arrived. He also anticipated sharing in spiritual refreshment with them during his visit and to enlist their participation in his mission campaign into the western Mediterranean, particularly to Spain.[52]

2. Sanctification: The Transforming of Life (5:1-8:39)

◇◇

5 Therefore, since we have been set right through faith, we have peace with God through our Lord Jesus Christ, [2]through whom also we have gained access by faith into this grace in which we now stand, and we boast in the hope of the glory of God. [3]Not only this, but we also exult in our sufferings, because we know that suffering produces patience; [4]patience, tested character; and proven character, hope. [5]And hope does not disappoint, because God's love has been poured out into our hearts through the Holy Spirit, who has been given to us. ⁶For while we were still powerless, at just the right time, Christ died for the ungodly. ⁷Rarely will anyone die for a righteous person, though perhaps for a good person someone might possibly dare to die. ⁸But God introduces his own love for us in this: while we were still sinners, Christ died for us! ⁹How much more then, having now been set right by his blood, shall we be saved from God's wrath through him! ¹⁰For if, while being God's enemies, we were reconciled to God through the death of his Son, how much more, having been reconciled, shall we be saved through his life! ¹¹But not only this, but we also boast in God through our Lord Jesus Christ, through whom we now have received this reconciliation.

In 5:1-11, Paul shifted his focus to include new evidence as he explained the blessings of justification. The hermeneutical principle of the "analogy of faith" comes through strongly in the closing verses of chapter four, which opens the way for being put right with God.[52] That is to say, Abraham trusted God, which is what God wanted. "Justification is God's proclamation that a person is righteous, and that makes it so."[53] The change is not only to a right relationship with God, but being set right, an internal, personal, moral change as well. This real change is called sanctification. These works of God for us and in us are the two grand branches of human salvation.

Now that Paul has laid the foundations for his explanation of the gospel, he will begin to bring out applications to the Christian life. Some of the blessings that justification brings we can enjoy now. Faith has appropriated grace (5:2) offered to us through the hand of Jesus. The opened human hand receives the free gift. More vigorously put, the flailing hand of a drowning victim has been grasped by the great Rescuer. If we do not resist, or panic further, but rest in the strength of the Savior, then it will be well with our soul. A result of trusting God is being at peace.[54] Of course, Paul is not advocating a purely passive attitude, but one of active engagement for Christian living. His emphasis is on the prior work and enablement of God as the basis for our response and resulting activity. It is entering into a relationship of wholeness and living life. You can feel the heartbeat of the letter in this section.[55]

Where, but in Rome, was it more likely to hear or be required to say, "Caesar is Lord"? They were aware of the Pax Romana, but Paul was talking about a different kind of peace and a greater Lord (Romans 10:9). His hearers would have keyed in upon these words and been eager to hear his explanation, as applied to Jesus and to themselves. Paul marked out Jesus as the true and risen Lord (Philippians 2:11; 1 Corinthians 12:3), and the peace Jesus brings is not a cessation of military conflict, but a heart restored, a relationship mended. "Righteousness and peace have kissed each other" (Psalms 85:10). "The effect of righteousness will be peace" (Isaiah 32:17). Both the Jewish and Gentile hearers would have caught the significance of this, albeit from different cultural backgrounds.

Paul moved into a succession of results available to those who stand in the grace of God through faith, "because God's love has been poured into our hearts through the Holy Spirit that has been given to us" (5:5). We are being renewed in the image of God! Christ did not just come to die for His friends, or the "good guys." "God demonstrates His love for us that while we were still sinners, Christ died for us" (5:1-8). This is the work of reconciliation, turning former enemies into friends.[56]

There is also joy in Christ. Even in tribulation because of faith in Christ, joy is present because of the presence of Christ in our lives, and living in this joy in the midst of trials produces Christian character. Character produced in this crucible of trial yields hope. Hope will not disappoint because of the presence of the Holy Spirit in our lives saturating our hearts with His love. The suffering servant of Isaiah and the imagery of the Pascal lamb of the Passover come together to interpret the meaning of Calvary. Here the meaning of reconciliation becomes most clear. God has provided for our reconciliation, because God has accomplished atonement in Christ. But reconciliation is not effective until it has removed our enmity toward God (5:9-11). "The death of Christ does not automatically provide salvation for the elect but makes available the possibility of salvation to all who respond in faith."[57]

◇◇◇

[12]Therefore, just as sin entered the world through one human, and death through sin, and in this way death spread to all people, because all sinned. [13]Sin was in the world before the Law, but sin was not reckoned against anyone's account where there is no Law, [14]nevertheless, death reigned from

Adam until Moses, even upon those who did not sin like the trespass of Adam, who is a type of the Coming One.

[15]But the grace gift is not like the trespass. For if through the trespass of the one, the many died, how much more did God's grace and the gift that came by the grace gift of the one man, Jesus Christ, abound to the many! [16]But the grace gift is not like the trespass: The judgment followed one sin and brought condemnation, but the grace gift followed many trespasses and brought acquittal. [17]For if, by the trespass of the one man, death reigned through that one man, how much more will those who receive God's abundant provision of grace and of the gift of righteousness reign in life through the one man, Jesus Christ!

[18]Consequently, just as one trespass resulted in condemnation for all people, so also one righteous act for all people for putting right life. [19]For just as through the disobedience of the one human the many were made sinners, so also through the obedience of the One many were constituted righteous.

[20]The Law was brought in so that the trespass might increase. But where sin increased, grace super-abounded, [21]so that, just as sin reigned in death, so also grace might reign through righteousness leading to everlasting life through Jesus Christ our Lord.

◇◇

In 5:12-21, Paul tackled the problem of sin from a different angle, using a comparison of Adam and Christ. He laid out his argument that the universal problem of sin has an available universal cure. However, a step along the way was to show sin for what it was, so that everyone would be aware of it. The Law was given so that sin could be seen as the evil it was and that humans could know that they could not undo it by themselves (5:20). The limb they sawed off was the one upon which they sat. There is no catching yourself and putting the limb back. It takes the act of God to catch the falling soul, re-graft the limb, and help us out of our hiding place in the tree to have open fellowship with God again.

More sure than "the soul that sins will die" is the provision that those who trust in Christ, shall live. The certainty of full salvation, in both time and eternity, is backed not only by Christ viewed as "the Christ of the cross," but by Christ viewed as the new *Adam*. Just as sin and death entered into the world through Adam's disobedience, Christ's obedience leads to life for all who believe. There needs to be no doubt that God's provision in Christ is fully sufficient for salvation. What Christ has done has universal validity. Not only has the relationship changed to "right standing," but God has begun to *transform* our inner nature and character by the work of the Holy Spirit.

Through this section of the letter, Paul brings out the ethical implications of justification by pointing to the work of the Spirit in us in sanctification. If justification is the work of Christ *for us* to restore a right relationship to God, then sanctification is the act of renewal *in us* to make us alive spiritually (regeneration). Sanctification, our inward and outward holiness, begins chronologically at the same time as the finished act of our justification, but continues as we "grow up in Him who is our Head."[58]

Paul can say, because he has met the risen Lord and believes, "If anyone is in Christ, he is a new creation; the old has passed away, behold the new has come." God has made a fresh beginning in Christ. Adam and Christ are the heads of two opposing orders of human existence. Adam's defection from God brought the reign of sin and death. The new order, initiated by Christ's redemptive act, is an order where grace reigns in righteousness leading to everlasting life. The spheres of Adam and Christ are death and life respectively. Paul is speaking of opposing powers. Adam represents human will opposed to the divine will, disobedient, hostile, and rebellious. In this broken order, sin governs our actions, a power leading us to death (cf. 7:9-11).

On the other hand, grace which reigns through Christ is also a power, a liberating force, which frees us from the power of sin and death (5:21). These two realms both claim humanity and vie for their allegiance. How we live our lives is determined by which one we choose. Our destiny hangs in the balance.

By nature, we are in Adam. Sin indwells us. Sin is a human fact before it is an individual act. This propensity to sin eventually provokes me to commit a personal transgression, and I join in solidarity with all the other sinners. The end result is death.

In contrast, by grace through faith we are in Christ, through whom we receive the free gift (5:18).

The world has been invaded by the power of grace to effect a new creation in Christ Jesus. What is the free gift? Life! God's grace enables us to accept the offer of this gift in Christ. It counteracts the guilt of inherited sin, and makes justification universally available. Abounding grace is ours in Christ not only in forgiveness of sins but in imparting holiness that leads to eternal life (5:20-21). What Paul has argued through his presentation in chapter five is that through Jesus Christ the sin that entered the human race and reigns in death is now provisionally expelled.

◇◇

6What then shall we say? Shall we continue to sin so that grace may increase? ²Of course not! For we have died to sin; how can we live in it? ³ Or do you not know that all of us who were baptized into Christ Jesus were baptized into his death? ⁴ We were buried then with him through baptism into death in order that, just as Christ was raised from the dead through the glory of the Father, we too may walk in newness of life. ⁵For if we have been joined in the likeness of his death, we will certainly also be joined with him in the likeness of his resurrection.

⁶For we know that our old self was crucified with him so that the body of death might be done away with, that we should no longer be slaves to sin. ⁷For the one who has died is freed from sin. ⁸But if we have died with Christ, we believe that we will also live with him. ⁹For we know that since Christ was raised from the

dead, he cannot die again; death no longer rules over him. [10]The death he died, he died to sin once for all; but the life he lives, he lives to God. [11]In the same way, then, reckon yourselves dead to sin but alive to God in Christ Jesus.

[12]Therefore do not let sin reign in your mortal body so that you obey its desires, [13]Do not lend any part of yourself to sin as an weapon of wickedness, but rather offer yourselves to God as those who have been brought from death to life; and present every part of yourself to him as an instrument of righteousness. [14]For sin will not rule you, because you are not under the Law, but under grace.

In Romans 6:1-6, Paul urged the hearers to put behind them their old life in terms of both actions and being, and to put on the new life, which is given content by the character of Christ. Sin is incompatible with the Christian life. This is Paul's premise for raising and answering the posed question.

"Spiritual maturation is both positive and negative. It is the ridding ourselves of all that is contrary to the mind of Christ and adding those virtues that are defined by the person of the Savior."[59] The believer shares in the baptism of Jesus (6:3-4) as a way of identifying with Christ. At Jesus' baptism, He has taken up the cross proleptically. He is inducted into the role of the Suffering Servant of Isaiah 53. Likewise, the believer is to acknowledge the nature of Christian baptism as a declaration of intent to "put to death" everything in one's life that is contrary to the will of God or antithetical to Christlikeness.[60]

For Paul, it is unthinkable for a Christian, a justified believer, to go on sinning, "for the declaration that grace reigns (5:21) is at the same time a declaration that sin's power has been broken."[61] Charles Wesley affirmed this poetically,

> He breaks the power of canceled sin,
> He sets the prisoner free,
> His blood can make the foulest clean;
> His blood availed for me.[62]

"How can we *as Christians* go on living in sin since we, *as Christians*, have died to sin?"[63] Where grace reigns, sin ceases (6:3-10). When we are converted to Christ, sin's reign comes to an end. We die with Christ and are raised to "newness of life." He makes the case that we should not continue **in** sin, first, and then presses the issue that we should not continue **to** sin. If we have known the power of sin in our lives, now Paul wants us to feel the stronger power of grace. There is no good reason to continue to commit sins.

◇◇◇

[15]What then? Shall we commit sin because we are not under the law but under grace? Of course not! [16]Do you not know that when you offer yourselves to someone as obedient slaves, you are slaves of the one you obey, whether sin, which leads to death, or obedience, which leads to righteousness? [17]But thanks be to God that, though you were slaves to sin, you have come to obey from your heart the

pattern of teaching that has now claimed you. [18]Being freed from sin you have become slaves to righteousness. [19](I am using a metaphor because of your human weakness.)

Just as you lent yourselves as slaves to impurity and to ever-increasing sinfulness, so now lend yourselves as slaves to righteousness leading to sanctification. [20]When you were slaves to sin, you were free from righteousness. [21]What fruit did you reap from the time spent in things you are now ashamed of? Those things result in death! [22]But now having been set free from sin and enslaved of God, the fruit you reap leads to sanctification, and the end product is eternal life. [23]For the wages of sin is death, but the grace-gift of God is eternal life in Christ Jesus our Lord.

Freed from sin's power to serve righteousness, the dominion of sin is traded for Christ's *Kingdominion*. A brief overview of chapter six says: where grace reigns, sin ceases (6:1-14); where sin is given a place in our lives, grace effectively is mitigated and death ensues (6:15-16). Standing before and under God is freedom. The power of sin is broken and the prisoner of sin and death is set free to be obedient to sanctification and righteousness (6:15-23).

John Wesley summed it up, "God works; therefore, you *can* work...God works; therefore, you *must* work."[64] Part of what this means was expressed by Paul in 6:19, "so present your members as slaves to righteousness, resulting in sanctification." Paul is calling the justified believer to entire consecration which will result in their entire sanctification.[65] Paul is presenting the idea that what must be removed is the illusion of self-sovereignty. When we finally present ourselves "as a living sacrifice" to Christ, as "slaves of righteousness," then we can be free from sin and fully alive to God, fully sanctified (cf. 1 Thessalonians 5:23-24). The contrast is clear: the due penalty for sin is death; accepting the free gift in Christ is life (6:23).

7Do you not know, brothers and sisters, for I am speaking to those who know what law is about, that law governs someone only as long as that person lives? [2]For example, by law a married woman is bound to her husband as long as he is alive, but if her husband dies, she is released from the law that binds her to him. [3]So then, while her husband is still alive, if she becomes joined to another man, she is an adulteress. But if her husband is dead, she is released from that law and is not an adulteress if she marries another man. [4]So then, my brothers and sisters, you also died to law through the body of Christ, in order that you might belong to another, to him who was raised from the dead, in order that we might bear fruit for God.

[5]For when we were in the flesh, the sinful passions aroused by the law were at work in us, so that we bore fruit for death. [6]But now, we have been released from the law

> by dying to what held us captive, so that
> we serve in the newness of the Spirit, and
> not in the old way of the letter.

In 7:1-6, Paul emphasized that being under grace means to be joined to the risen Christ in covenant love. "My brothers and sisters, you have died to the law through the body of Christ, so that you belong to another, to him who has been raised from the dead in order that we may bear fruit for God" (7:4). The possibility of making room for sin is excluded. Here Paul argued that we are set free from the law at the same time we are set free from sin. "When we had nothing but the Law, we were at the mercy of sin."[66]

> [7]What then shall we say? Is the Law sin? Of course not! But, I would not have known sin except through the Law, for I would not have known what coveting was if the Law had not said, "You shall not covet." [8]But sin, taking the opportunity through the commandment, produced in me all sorts of desire, for apart from the Law, sin was dead. [9]I was alive apart from the Law at one time, but when the commandment came, sin sprang to life and I died. [10]I found that the very commandment that was intended to bring life actually brought me death. [11]For sin, taking the opportunity through the commandment, deceived me, and killed me through it. [12]So then, the Law is holy, and the commandment is holy, just and

> good. [13]Did the good, then, become death
> to me? Of course not! Nevertheless, sin,
> in order to reveal itself as sin, used what is
> good to bring about my death, so that sin
> might become utterly sinful through the
> commandment.

In this section and the next, Paul employs a rhetorical device known as impersonation telling Adam's tale.[67] Paul's point also included conveying the function of the Law (7:7-13). Sin works through the Law, because the Law makes clear the code of conduct and what sin is. The example of Adam and the Fall found in Genesis is how Paul explains this concept in the text. Since humanity rebelled against God and gave sin dominion over the self, the Law enforces the standard of righteousness that we do not keep in our sin-prone, self-centered condition. Paul rejects the foundation of code-keeping (which was misunderstood as the case for righteousness by the Jews and other moral people in general) for love-keeping, just as God originally intended. (As a side note—love will not violate, or misuse the relationships with others for selfish purposes. The issue at hand is "the believer's behavior and quality of life before God."[68] Love, not law, becomes the motive of his life.) The point being explained here specifically is about "a more universal tale of the progenitor of all humankind and then the story of all those "in Adam."[69]

> [14]We know that the Law is spiritual; but
> I am unspiritual, sold under sin. [15]I do
> not understand what I do. For I do not
> practice what I want to do, but what I hate

I do. ¹⁶And if I do not do what I want to do, I agree that the Law is good. ¹⁷But now it is no longer I myself who does it, but the sin which dwells within me. ¹⁸For I know that nothing good dwells in me, that is, in my sinful nature. For I have the will to do what is good, but I cannot do it. ¹⁹For I do not do the good I want to do, but the evil I do not want to do—this I practice. ²⁰But if I do not wish to do this, and nevertheless do it, then it is sin living in me that does it.

²¹Therefore, I find this law at work with my wanting to do good, evil is right there with me. ²²For I rejoice in God's Law in my inner self. ²³But I see another law at work in my members, waging war against the law of my mind and making me a captive of the law of sin at work within my members. ²⁴What a wretched human I am! Who will deliver me from the body of this death? ²⁵Thanks be to God through Jesus Christ our Lord! So then, on the one hand I myself in my mind am a slave to God's Law, but on the other hand in my sinful nature a slave to the law of sin.

In this controversial section (7:14-25), Paul is not explaining his present Christian experience, nor describing normative Christian experience at-large. That interpretation would disrupt the flow of his arguments describing the function of the Law and how sin works. He is continuing in the same vein of the argument begun in the previous section (7:7-13) as an Adamic soliloquy.[70] The current section brings the past

R. JEFFREY HIATT | 57

into the present and makes it personal for everyone, especially the person who wants to live a moral life in their own strength. Trying to live according to the letter of the law or conscience, the individual is aware that there is an inner conflict leading the opposite way. There is an inescapable bondage to doing wrong. Paul has made a convincing case for the impossibility of being righteous on one's own.

In summary, the thrust of the argument put forward in (7:1-6) is that death to sin means that we are also free **from** the law, as a basis for our justification or sanctification. It means, in a positive way, that we are under grace, free **for** God. The old sinful self has died and the "wife" is free to marry again: righteousness as a new creature in Christ Jesus. As long as sin is alive in us, we are bound (married) to the sinful self and under the Law. Death with Christ sets us free from the Law and sin. If we obey our new master, that is, the enabling grace of Christ, it makes possible a sanctifying union with the living resurrected Christ. The unaided self cannot experience, or achieve this type of life. It is only possible in Christ through the indwelling Holy Spirit. Paul explained both the history of sin and the function of the Law (7:7-13). Then, he made it personal to indict all people everywhere over their failure to live above sin (7:14-25). The point is that the Law is powerless to produce a sanctified life, a real change in the heart. Paul, the Pharisee, was found persecuting Christ with the intention of keeping the letter of the Law and trying to do the will of God! This sets the stage for his claims in Christ delivered in chapter eight.

With excitement and anticipation, in 8:1-39, Paul capped off his arguments explicating "the problem of the Law and its servitude to sin to [focus on] the power (the work of the Spirit applying the work of Christ to the believer) which saves the believer from the law and sin, and represents the foretaste of the promise of God's final victory over the powers of evil."[71]

Paul spoke of sharing in the Spirit with the Roman Church in his opening address (1:11-12). After laying a solid foundation of what it does not mean, as well as his understanding of Christ, he drew out why it is possible. This gives teeth to what Paul meant in the letter's theme 1:16-17, dealing with righteousness and its implications for the life of a believer. What has happened is that God has pronounced the guilty sinner pardoned (justified, rectified) and free from the rule of sin! That, however, is only half the story—the objective side. Now Paul is going to describe the experiential side, the inner transformation of the heart in life in the Spirit.[72]

8 So there is now no condemnation for those who are in Christ Jesus, [2]because through Christ Jesus the rule of the Spirit who gives life has set you free from the rule of sin and death. [3]For what the Law could not do because it was weakened by the flesh, God did by sending his own Son in the likeness of sinful flesh, and concerning sin, he condemned sin in the flesh, [4]in order that the righteous decree of the Law might be fulfilled in us, who walk not according to the flesh but according to the Spirit.

[5]Those who are according to the flesh set their minds on the things of the flesh, but those who are according to the Spirit, the things of the Spirit. [6]The mentality of the flesh is death, but the mentality of the Spirit is life and peace [7]because the mind governed by the flesh is enmity toward God, for it does not submit to God's Law, nor can it do so. [8]Those who are in the flesh cannot please God.

[9]You, however, are not in the flesh but in the Spirit, if indeed the Spirit of God lives in you. But if anyone does not have the Spirit of Christ, they do not belong to him. [10]But if Christ is in you, then even though your body is subject to death because of sin, the Spirit gives life because of righteousness. [11]But if the Spirit of him who raised Jesus from the dead is dwelling in you, he who raised Christ from the dead will even give life to your mortal body through his Spirit who dwells in you.

[12]Therefore, brothers and sisters, we are debtors, not to the flesh, to live according to it. [13]For if you live according to the flesh, you will die, but if by the Spirit you put to death the misdeeds of the body, you will live.

◇◇◇

The resonating tone in this section is life, life in the Spirit (8:1-13).[73] "Here both a future gift and a present grace merge with each other...Through the risen Lord we have received even now the quickening power of the Holy Spirit…Salvation is therefore more than a matter of the soul; salvation touches the whole man[sic], body and soul, both here and hereafter."[74]

The implication regarding sanctification is: "All believers, being sanctified by the Holy Spirit, are recipients of the Spirit" (see also 1 Corinthians 6:11).[75] The Spirit who flows from Christ reproduces Him in us. We have an inner allegiance to Christ. In fact, "becoming a believer" is the gift of the Spirit that makes this true (see Romans 8:9; Galatians 4:6; 1 Thessalonians 1:4-6; Philippians 2:1).[76] The Spirit "who raised Christ Jesus from the dead will give life to your mortal bodies also through his Spirit which dwells in you" (Romans 8:11). The outcome is seen in ethical terms whose content is the character of Christ; the experience of the Spirit is identified with the experience of the indwelling Christ.[77] The transformation is not only anticipated for individuals but for the world in which they live.[78] Paul is also affirming the reformation of the body in that it will no longer serve evil desires, but serve the new order of righteousness. It is the Spirit that has broken the power of canceled sin and set the prisoner free[79] to pursue God in obedience and love.

[14]For those who are led by the Spirit of God are children of God. [15]For you did not receive a spirit of slavery again unto fear; but you received, a Spirit of adoption, in whom we cry, *"Abba,* Father." [16]The Spirit himself bears witness with our spirit that we are God's children. [17]But if we are children, then we are heirs: heirs of God

and fellow heirs with Christ, if, that is, we
suffer with him so that we may be glorified
with him.

◇◇

The witness of the Spirit to us is assuring us of
our adoption as God's own dear children (8:14-17).[80]
A primary emphasis is the "witness of the Spirit."
Romans 8:16 puts it, "It is the Spirit himself bearing
witness with our spirit that we are children of God."
Being united with God brings about so thorough a
change in status that we experience the personal
internal, intimate connection to God through Christ
and the indwelling Spirit without fear.[81]

"To be a member of God's family means one shares
with others a common life shared in mutual
interdependence."[82] Here we can envision the picture
of Rublev's Icon of the Trinity.

Image 7: Russian
icon of the
Old Testament
Trinity by Andrey
Rublev (Андрéй
Рублёв), between
1408-1425.

We are drawn into the life of God and are given a seat at the table in fellowship with God and the rest of His family. This is the privilege of all Christians.

There is at the same time a confidence and humility characterizing the life of the Christian. "Such a unity within God's family is finally the solution to the problem of the hate-filled divisions of humanity," but before the transformation is finalized those who become part of the family will be rejected and persecuted by some of those who refuse to believe.[83] What should be grasped, however, is that even in the face of such difficulties, for those who trust Christ, the Spirit enacts the Good News in them, and they "are empowered by the vivifying presence of the Spirit to walk in newness of life."[84] Our heartfelt response to the One who has given us life by setting us "free from the law of sin and death" is to express to God the Spirit a loving attitude of gratitude, resulting in actions consistent with this commitment and feeling. The suffering for the cause of Christ is also a mark of those who are on their way to being glorified with him.

◇◇◇

[18]I reckon that our present sufferings are not worth comparing to the coming glory that will be revealed in us. [19]For the eager expectation of creation awaits the revelation of the children of God. [20]For the creation was subjected to frustration, not willingly, but by the will of the One who subjected it, in hope [21]that the creation itself will be freed from its slavery to decay and brought into the freedom of the glory of the children of God.

²²We know that the whole creation groans together as in the pains of childbirth up to the present time. ²³But not only so, but we ourselves, who have the first fruits of the Spirit, groan in ourselves awaiting adoption to sonship, the redemption of our bodies. ²⁴For we were saved in hope, but hope that is seen is no hope at all. Who hopes for what they already see? ²⁵ But if we hope for what we do not yet see, we wait for it patiently.

²⁶In the same way, the Spirit helps us in our weakness for we do not know how we ought to pray, but the Spirit himself intercedes for us through unspoken groans. ²⁷And the one who searches the heart knows the mind of the Spirit, so that in accordance with the will of God he intercedes for the saints.

²⁸And we know that for those who love God, all things work together for good, for those called according to his purpose. ²⁹For those whom he knew beforehand, he also destined beforehand to share the image of his Son, that he might be the firstborn among many brothers and sisters. ³⁰Those he destined beforehand, he also called; those he called, he also set right; those he set right, he also glorified.

In 8:18-30, the theme of Christian hope rises to the surface. There is no need for worry, but the work of love in the heart also boldly propels the believer

ahead in both growth and service. Staying in step with the Spirit, Paul reassured the believer that the present salvation will continue and be connected to the final resurrection (Romans 8:23). Although there may be persecution in the present scope of things, the future glory will far outweigh any inconvenience, suffering, or any other evil thrust upon the one who trusts God. There will be a vindication. In the present, however, they are called to hold onto the promise in hope, which will be fulfilled just as sure as Jesus is who he said he was. This means, in part, that God will also restore his violated creation to its original pristine-type goodness (cf. Ephesians 1:10; Colossians 1:20).[85]

◇◇

[31]What, then, shall we say to these things? If God is for us, is anyone against us? [32]He who did not even spare his own Son, but delivered him up for us all, how will he not also, along with him, graciously give us all things? [33]Who will bring any accusation against those whom God has chosen? It is God who sets it right. [34]Who will condemn? Christ Jesus is the one who died, and more than that, who was raised to life, who is at the right hand of God and is also interceding for us. [35]What shall separate us from the love of Christ? Will suffering or distress or persecution or famine or nakedness or danger or sword? [36]Just as it is written: "For your sake we face death all day long; we are regarded as sheep to be slaughtered." [37]But in all these situations we prevail completely through

> him who loved us. [38]For I am convinced
> that neither death nor life, neither angels
> nor rulers, neither things present nor
> things to come, nor powers, [39]nor height
> nor depth, nor anything else in all creation,
> will be able to separate us from the love of
> God that is in Christ Jesus our Lord.

In Romans 8:31-39 we hear echoes of 1 Corinthians 13 as Paul points us to the love of God for the motivation behind all of the preceding material. As Paul brought this section to completion, he wanted there to be no mistake, or lack of clarity, of what lay behind all of this. There is no good reason to fear. God has mobilized all of the resources of heaven to help every human being. There is nothing in all of creation that can stop a person who truly trusts in Christ. God's juggernaut love toward all of us, toward each of us, is settled. Jesus is the demonstration of God's love toward us, and the Spirit in us is the evidence of what is to come.

We should not take Paul's indication of the process of salvation in the list of terms he strings together as a repudiation of being "saved by grace through faith." This does not mean that God is the one who does the trusting of God and we are just along for the ride. Salvation is not based on God's arbitrary decision of who is *in* and who is *out*. That would undermine what he had written in the preceding part of the letter. Paul was giving a glimpse of the overview of God's design. This is what can be trusted. This is what should be and what is available to every person who trusts Christ. His meaning is to give us complete confidence in what God is doing. This does not exclude the human response and responsibility; to do so would violate being made in the image of God.[86] God is completely trustworthy, and you are safe in His hands. Paul meant, "Don't doubt it for a minute!" Nothing can take God's love from you; however, this does not mean that *you* cannot throw it away. But no one can take it against your will.

As Paul began this chapter on the note of assurance, he closed with a Hallelujah Chorus resounding in his listeners ears. This movement of Paul's symphony-in-words crescendos with rapturous strands of exuberant exultation!

C. God's Righteousness: Obtained by Faith (9:1-11:36)

In the three chapters nine through eleven, Paul is ringing a clarion call about salvation-by-faith or righteousness-by-faith.[87] Through these chapters, Paul leaves no room for any other way to God but by responding to the grace given to us as faith or trust in Christ. He wants to drive this idea home. The history of Israel shows that the rebellious among them or among her neighbors faced the same consequences (cf. Amos, et. al). Trust the Lord, receive His mercy, and live (cf. Jonah). Serve idols (reject God), incur God's wrath, and die. Paul sought purposely to remove the wedge between Jewish and Gentile believers on this issue. God's patient grace has not changed.

Paul's personal passion for the gospel comes out in this public display of intensity over the importance of what he is saying. He brought to climax the importance of seeing the continuity of the Jews as an integral part of God's continuing plan to reach all people with the message of reconciliation. To miss the importance of these chapters is to truncate Paul's driving thrust of chapters 1-8 as well.

This section is not a minor triplet tacked on at the end of his great chorus. Paul has worked diligently to defend his gospel and anchor it to the principles of Scripture and show how Jesus rightly interprets the long history of God's involvement with Israel. Paul clarified the debate between Judaism and the church. Since the Roman Christians faced these same issues, Paul made it plain what the proper gospel stance was.[88]

Paul's aim was to resolve these tensions: 1) The Jews, on a large scale, are not experiencing the salvation offered in Christ (9:1-3); 2) Although they have had many privileges (9:4-5); 3) By God's electing love they were chosen to share God's love and mission, but from the standpoint of rejecting the gospel, they are "enemies," found fighting against God (11:28). Paul, himself, is at the center of this controversy. He advocated and explained: 1) Jews are not guaranteed salvation through the Mosaic covenant (chapter two), so what does "chosen people (Deuteronomy 7:6)" mean? 2) What does the "promise" to the Jew and the Gentile actually entail? 3) If the Jew rejects and the Gentile accepts the gospel what does that mean? Paul saw that to jettison the Jews was to undermine the gospel. God must be shown to be faithful and trustworthy in order for the gospel to be believed by anyone. God is not inconsistent. What God has said in the past, which was given in Scripture, is in line with what He is currently doing in Christ and the church. God has fully provided for Israel while demonstrating His love for the entire world.[89]

In John Wesley's *Explanatory notes on the New Testament*, he summarizes the chapter,

> In this chapter, St. Paul, after strongly declaring his love and esteem for them, sets himself to answer the grand objection of his countrymen; namely, that the rejection of the Jews and reception of the gentiles was contrary to the word of God. That he had not here the least thought of personal election or reprobation is manifest, because it lay quite wide of his design, which was this, to show that God's rejecting the Jews and receiving the gentiles was consistent with his word because such a doctrine would not only have had no tendency to convince, but would have evidently tended to harden, the Jews; because when he sums up his argument in the close of the chapter, he has not one word, or the least intimation, about it.[90]

Paul presented the universality of the gospel through the entire letter. He established that Jew and Gentile are on equal footing before God (all have sinned!) and need God's mercy. Next, he aimed to produce a unity among Jewish and Gentile believers.[91]   This is why he continued to deny that God has completely rejected the Jews (Romans 11:1). Again, anyone may be saved by grace through faith. Just because the mission of the Kingdom is taken from Israel and given to the Church does not mean that there is any room for anti-Semitism, nor are there two paths for salvation (see also Luke 6:46ff). (Think of Jesus' parable of the two servants in Luke 12:41-48, or the Vineyard Tenants in Mark 12:1-12.)

Paul understood personally the reality that the offer of salvation is through faith in Christ. It is the same for Jew and Gentile "without distinction and unrelated to national origin."[92] There is one people of God, whose continuity is directly related to God's redemptive purposes.[93] The aim of the new look of the olive tree is a new unity of all the redeemed (Jew and Gentile), that is, those who trust in Christ (11:20).[94]

9 I am telling the truth in Christ, I am not lying, as my conscience bears witness to me through the Holy Spirit, [2]that it is a great sorrow and ceaseless anguish in my heart. [3]For I could pray that I myself were accursed and separated from Christ for the sake of my people, my kindred according to the flesh, [4]who are the people of Israel. They are the adoption to sonship; theirs is the glory, the covenants, the testimony of the Law, the worship and the promises, [5]whose are the patriarchs, and from whom came the human ancestry of the Messiah, who above all is God, forever praised! Amen.

[6]It is not, of course, that the Word of God had failed, for not all who are descended from Israel are Israel. [7]Nor is it the case that all Abraham's descendants are all children, but in Isaac that your offspring will be reckoned." [8]In other words, it is not the children by physical descent who are God's children, but it is the children of the promise who are reckoned as Abraham's seed. [9]For this is the word of the promise: "At the appointed time I will come, and Sarah shall have a son."

[10]But not only that, but also Rebekah's children were conceived at the same time by our ancestor Isaac. [11]Yet, before the twins were born or had done anything good or bad—in order that God's plan/ purpose remain according to free choice/ election: [12]not from works but by the calling—she was told, "The older will serve the younger," [13]just as it is written: "Jacob I loved, but Esau I hated."

[14]What then shall we say? Is there injustice/unrighteousness with God? Not ever! [15]For he says to Moses, "I will have mercy on whom I have mercy, and I will have compassion/pity on whom I will have compassion/pity." [16]Therefore, it is not the one who wills, nor the one who runs, but it is of God's mercy. [17]For the Scripture says to Pharaoh: "I raised you up for this very thing, that I might show my power in you and that my name might be proclaimed in all the earth." [18]Therefore, he has mercy

on whom he wills to have mercy, and he hardens whom he wills to harden.

[19]You then will say to me: "Why then is there any blame? For who can resist his will?" [20]But who are you, a mere human being, to talk back to God? "What is molded say to the one who formed it, 'Why have you made me this way?'" [21]Does not the potter have the authority to make out of the same lump of clay some pottery for honorable purposes and some for common use? [22]But What if God, although wishing to show his wrath and make his power known, bore with great patience the objects of his wrath who have been preparing themselves for destruction, [23]and in order that he might make known the riches of his glory to the vessels of his mercy, whom he prepared in advance for glory, [24]even us, whom he also called, not only from the Jews but also from the Gentiles/nations, [25]as it even says in Hosea: "I will call them 'my people' who are not my people; and she who is not my beloved, my beloved;" [26]and, "In the very place where it was said to them, 'You are not my people,' there they will be called 'children of the living God.'" [27]But Isaiah cries out concerning Israel: "Even if the number of the Israelites be like the sand of the sea, those left behind/the remnant will be saved. [28]For the Lord will carry out his sentence on earth, completing it but limiting it." [29]It is just as Isaiah foretold: "Unless the Lord Almighty/Sabaoth had

left to us seed, we would become like
Sodom, and become like Gomorrah."

30What then shall we say? The Gentiles,
who did not pursue righteousness, attained
righteousness based on faith? 31But Israel,
pursuing a law of righteousness in the
Law, have not attained their goal? 32Why
not? Because they pursued it not by faith
but as if it were on the basis of works.
They stumbled on the stumbling stone,
33just as it is written: "Behold, I place in
Zion a stone of stumbling and a rock of
offense, and the one believing in him will
not be put to shame."

Paul pours out his open heart of compassion for
those of his ethnic identity (9:1-5). He pleads with
them to cast themselves upon God's mercy, since
it extends to them. But lest they thought God's
mercy was an exclusive disposition toward them, he
disproves this misconception and elucidated God's
mercy toward all people, everywhere.

Paul previously made the case that Abraham was
not a Jew when God counted his trust in the Almighty
as righteousness (Romans 5:1-11). The seal and sign
of this trust was circumcision, the promise of Isaac,
and becoming the father of nations, including others
not intended to be part of this missionary people.
The Jews have had the historical blessings of the Law
and the Prophets, the Temple, and God's abiding
Glory. Paul remembered their history and both God's
faithfulness and their ambivalent behavior.

As a whole group, they were selected on behalf of the world to bring the Messiah to the world (9:7-18). This is in line with 1 Peter 2:9-10: "But you are a chosen race, a royal priesthood, a holy nation, God's own people **that** you may declare the wonderful deeds of him who called you out of darkness into his marvelous light" (my emphasis). They did nothing to merit this selection. Jacob was the chosen line of physical descent through whom the promise would be fulfilled, thus, "Jacob I loved." Esau was not the one chosen for this purpose, thus, the designation "Esau I hated." This does not mean saved and damned![95] Jacob was chosen for this purpose, for this mission. Jacob was the vessel of high honor. Esau was chosen for common purposes. But, disobedience is not excused in either case. This is irrevocable; it is history. "God will have mercy on whom he will have mercy;" that is, God is merciful to all (9:18). God is faithful.

Pharaoh is used in this same light. In the contest of "wills" as to who is the real God, God was shown as more able, stronger. God stiffens and hardens Pharaoh's heart, but not against Pharaoh's own will! (But, if Pharaoh was god as he claimed, then how could God do anything to Him?) God made Pharaoh abide by the stiff-necked choice he made. God demonstrated His love in redemption toward Israel and his judgment upon the rebellious Egyptians (9:17-18).[96]

God has the right to use his creation in any way His loving, holy character (that is, His very nature) allows (9:19-29). The story of the potter and clay carry the same meaning as that of Jacob and Esau, demonstrating God's mercy and love. What has not changed is that both Israel and the church are called into existence by the activity of God.[97] The difference was that the Jews remained oriented toward a national life; whereas, these new believers were constituted as the people of God through faith in Christ and the life-giving Holy Spirit.

Paul is helping Jewish and Gentile believers see this new unifying focus that they were one people in the Spirit (Romans 8), made righteous on the basis of faith/trust in God through Christ. Now showing God's heart for all of creation, and even using ambivalent Israel, God has made salvation more vividly known to all through His Son Jesus, the Faithful One. In him, all of the promises to Abraham have pointed. The Jews were not forgotten, but no one is saved against their will. God is lovingly sovereign, not capricious, nor arbitrary. God is merciful to all. God is faithful.

What Paul decisively had to show was: 1) that God has not forsaken his first chosen people (9:1-29), 2) that the Word of God has not failed (9:1-13), and 3) that all Israel has not permanently stumbled and been lost (9:30-10:4), since this would undermine Christian confidence in God as trustworthy.[98] God's salvation plan cannot be and is not based on national identity or ethnic superiority. It is rooted in His compassion and mercy. Israel is still a part of God's plan, just the same. The crux of the matter hinges on faith for either Jew or Gentile (9:30-33).[99] The promises always are conditional, rooted in God's grace and accepted through our trust in Christ.

When God gives grace, enabled by God's action, the human response is trust (10:1-13).[100] There is no behavior that earns God's decision to make us right with Him. That would put God in our debt. This was the approach the Jewish people had taken with the Law in their unenlightened zeal.[101] "In setting out to merit God's grace, they ignored that grace and shifted the area of trust from God's goodness to their own goodness" (10-1-3).[102] The Gentile saw the cross and was content to be in God's debt.

◇◇◇◇◇◇◇◇◇◇◇◇◇◇◇◇◇◇◇◇◇◇◇◇◇◇◇◇◇◇◇◇◇◇◇

10 Brothers and sisters, my heart's desire and my petition to God for them is for salvation. [2]For I bear witness about them that they have a zeal for God, but it is not based on knowledge. [3]Failing to recognize the righteousness of God and seeking to establish their own, they did not submit to God's righteousness. [4]Christ is the end of the Law so that there may be righteousness for everyone who believes. [5]For Moses writes this about the righteousness from the law: "The person who does these things will live in them." [6]But the righteousness that is by faith says: "Do not say in your heart, 'Who will ascend into heaven?'" (that is, to bring Christ down) [7]"or 'Who will descend into the deep?'" (that is, to bring Christ up from the dead). [8]But what does it say? "The word is near you; it is in your mouth and in your heart." This is, the word of faith that we proclaim: [9]If you confess with your mouth, "Jesus is Lord," and believe in your heart that God raised him from the dead, you will be saved. [10]For you believe in your heart unto righteousness, but you confess with your mouth for salvation. [11]As Scripture says, "Anyone believing in him will not be put to shame." [12]For there is no distinction between Jews and Gentiles, the same Lord is Lord of all, bestowing his riches upon all who call on him, [13]for, "Everyone who calls on the name of the Lord shall be saved."

Paul reasoned that, those who trust in God are Jews, and those who do not trust Him are not Jews, regardless of ethnic identity. It just does not have anything to do specifically with physical traits and ancestral linage, or national identity. Faith produces "Jews," real believers. "Gentiles are being included in God's true spiritual people, because they are experiencing the former positive kind of righteousness, a righteousness that is now available to anyone who believes (10:4b, 11-13)."[103] What Paul is calling for is faith as the human response to the revealed divine will.[104] Christ is the demonstration of God's faithfulness to His creation, as the incarnation is the goal of the Law (10:6-13).[105] "Christ has put an end to any other means of righteousness for believers, whether we mean by that right standing, sanctification, moral behavior, or final righteousness."[106]

[14]How, then, can they call on the one in whom they have not believed? And how shall they believe in the one of whom they have not heard? And how can they hear without preaching? [15]And how can anyone preach unless they have been sent? As it is written: "How beautiful are the

feet of those who proclaim the good news!" [16]But not all obey the proclamation. For Isaiah says, "Lord, who has believed our message?" [17]For, faith comes from hearing, but hearing through the word about Christ. [18]But I ask: Have they not heard? Indeed they did: "Unto all the earth their voice has gone out, their words to the ends of the inhabited world." [19]Again I ask: Did Israel not understand? First, Moses says, "I will make you jealous by those who are not a nation; a nation that has no understanding will make you angry." [20]And Isaiah boldly says, "I was found among those who did not seek me; I revealed myself to those who did not ask for me." [21]But concerning Israel he says, "All day long I have stretched out my hands to a disobedient and obstinate people."

In 10:14-21, the centerpiece is that faith is produced by listening to the teachings of Christ (10:17). Faith becomes the inner life of the heart, and finds expression in our outer of word and deed (10:9-10), or what Wesley called "works of piety" and "works of mercy." "Faith works in the heart to produce righteousness."[107] One's total life is built around trusting God. That loving trust is active.

In these verses, we see our need for repentance and self-examination to show that our relationship with God is based upon His grace, His trustworthiness. We accept his work (for us, in us, and through us) and respond in gratitude and service.[108] In this section, Paul anchored his reason for his own missionary travels. Those who have not heard the message of Christ need to hear in order to respond to the full revelation in Christ. He was one of the "sent ones" for that purpose. Love calls forth a response: "Here am I, send me" (Isaiah 6:8).

In chapter eleven, Paul pressed the case for why God has not rejected Israel, why God is trustworthy, and why his audience can have confidence in Him. Not all Jews reject(ed) God, and not all Gentiles (will) accept, but for those who do, it will be on the basis of grace through faith/trust, and they will be a part of the same living organism (10:16-21).[109] Paul gave himself as part of the evidence: a Jew, yet, a believer in Christ.

11 I ask then: Did God push away his people? Of course not! I am an Israelite myself, a descendant of Abraham, from the tribe of Benjamin. [2]God has not rejected his people, whom he foreknew. Don't you know what Scripture says in the passage about Elijah about how he appealed to God against Israel: [3]"Lord, they have killed your prophets and torn down your altars; I am the only one left, and they seek my life?"? [4]And what does God say to him? "I have reserved for myself seven thousand who have not bowed the knee to Baal." [5]So then, in the present time there is a remnant according to the free choice by grace. [6]And if by grace, then it cannot be based on works; if it were, grace would no longer be grace.

Paul drew on the story of Elijah who did God's will and work in faith. Although Elijah was rejected by much of the people, yet there was a faithful remnant. This fulfillment keeps the story alive, and God keeps the story alive in them! God is merciful. God is faithful. This truth is repeated down the corridors of time. Paul could still hear it and beckoned for those around him to hear it as well (11:1-6).

>⁷What then? What Israel sought they did not attain, but the chosen among them did. But the others were hardened, ⁸as it is written: "God gave them a spirit of stupor, eyes that could not see and ears that could not hear, to this very day." ⁹And David says: "May their table become a snare and a trap, a stumbling block and a retribution for them. ¹⁰May their eyes be darkened so they cannot see, and their backs be bent over forever."
>
>¹¹Again I say: Have they stumbled so as to fall beyond recovery? Of course not! Rather, because of their false step, salvation has come to the Gentiles to make Israel jealous. ¹²But if their trespass means riches for the world, and their failure means riches for the Gentiles, how much greater riches will their full number bring!

Think of the stories about the older and younger brothers in the Bible: Cain and Abel, Isaac and Ishmael, Jacob and Esau, Joseph and his brothers, or Jesus' parable of the Loving Father and the rebellious two sons. This is a common theme in scripture, that the older often is resentful of the younger.

In Jesus' parable, old Israel stands in the place of the older brother; the Gentile and Jewish believers in Christ are the younger brother. Their faith is to provoke the older brother to be jealous enough to come to faith as well (11:7-12).[110]

It is the custom to expect the older brother to be the mature and responsible one who leads the rest of his siblings by example and personal aid. The mystery that Paul detailed was that wisdom has come out of the mouth of the younger one to lead the older. Paul envisions, however, a reconciliation similar to that of Joseph and his brothers! It is incumbent upon the Gentile believers to be the example of faith that God longs for all people, including currently disobedient and obstinate Israel.

◇◇◇

[13]Now I am speaking to you Gentiles. Inasmuch as I am the apostle to the Gentiles, I am honoring my ministry, [14]if in some way to make my own people jealous and save some of them. [15]For if their rejection brought reconciliation to the world, what will their acceptance mean, if not life from the dead?

[16]If the first fruits are holy, then so is the whole mass of them; if the root is holy, so are the branches. [17]If some of the branches have been broken off, and you, though a wild olive branch, have been grafted in among the others and now share in the

nourishing sap from the olive root, [18]do not boast that you are superior to those other branches. If you do boast, consider this: You do not support the root, but the root supports you. [19]You will say then, "Branches were broken off so that I could be grafted in." [20]Very well. But they were broken off because of unfaith, and you stand by faith. Do not be haughty, but fear. [21]For if God did not spare the natural branches, is it likely that he will spare you?

[22]Behold the kindness and severity of God: severity to those who fell, but kindness to you, provided that you continue in his kindness. Otherwise, you also will be cut off. [23]And if they do not persist in unbelief, they will be grafted back in, for God is able to graft them in again. [24]After all, if you were cut out of an olive tree that is wild by nature, and contrary to nature were grafted into a cultivated olive tree, how much more readily will these, the natural branches, be grafted into their own olive tree!

[25]I do not want you to be ignorant of this mystery, brothers and sisters, so that you may not be conceited. Israel has experienced a hardening in part until the full number of the Gentiles has come in, [26]and in this way all Israel will be saved as it is written: "The deliverer will come from Zion; he will turn godlessness away from Jacob. [27]And this shall be my covenant with them when I take away their sins."

[28]As far as the gospel is concerned, they are enemies for your sake; but as far as election is concerned, they are loved on account of the patriarchs. [29]For God's grace gift and his call are irrevocable. [30]Just as you who were at one time disobedient to God have now received mercy because of their disobedience, [31]so they too have now become disobedient in order that they too may now receive mercy as a result of God's mercy to you. [32]For God has shut up everyone unto disobedience so that he may have mercy on them all.

[33]Oh, the depth of the riches of the wisdom and knowledge of God! How unsearchable his judgments, and his paths beyond tracing out! [34]"Who has known the mind of the Lord? Or who has been his counselor?" [35]"Who has ever given to God, that God should repay them?" [36]Because from him and through him and for him are all things. Glory to him forever. Amen.

God is the Gardener of the vineyard, and he can graft in whatever living branch he desires. Paul was blunt: God breaks off dead branches (11:17-24)! Don't be full of pride or you too could be caught dead in faith and broken off.[111] All were disobedient, but now God has made His mercy known to all (v. 31-32). This allows Gentiles to be part of the salvation plan! Then, the opportunity for faith is offered again to all Israel. Regardless of how one wants to understand "all Israel," Paul specified through the entire letter, the basis of coming to God is by grace through faith in Christ. Christ is the full revelation of God. He is "the Way, the Truth, and the Life." Nowhere does Paul contradict this, but only affirms it. Any interpretation of his words must conform to these basic parameters of the gospel. With relentless, steady pursuit (see the book of Hosea), God sought Israel—and Paul exclaimed, all Gentiles, too! This is the love of Christ to us.[112]

Paul's vision, however, saw this as the "blooming of the olive tree." That is, when many Jews come to faith in Christ, this will be a sign of Christ's return at the end of the age.[113] In Thessalonians, he foretold the great falling away before the end would come, but here he was writing of a great gathering in. With this denouement, Paul cemented the unity of the people of God as one people, who love and adore Him because of His mercy and grace toward all. With this admission in mind, Paul concluded this part of the letter with reverential and exuberant praise to God for his goodness and mercy to everyone (v.36)![114] From this cascade of grace, Paul launched into the next section, in order to show what this means practically in the lives of those who hear and respond to the gospel. A changed heart results in a changed life and lifestyle, however, this change is *not* automatic.

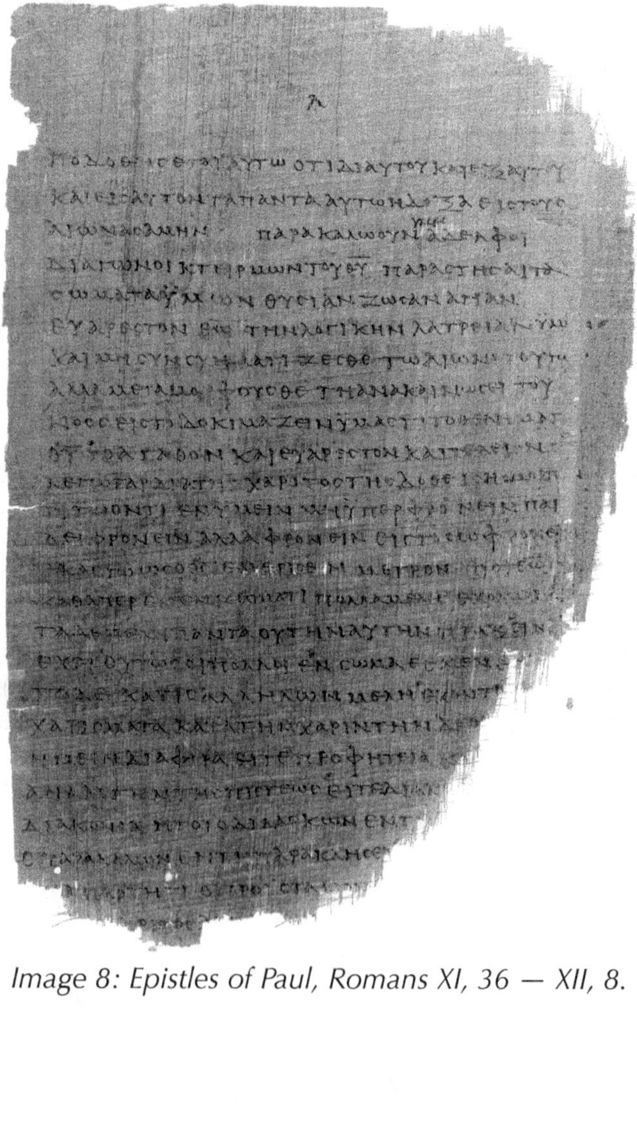

Image 8: Epistles of Paul, Romans XI, 36 — XII, 8.

III. Christian Formation (12:1-15:13)

In this section of Romans, Paul begins the work of constructing the Christian Community from the basic doctrines of the first eleven chapters. Paul sets the table of the Lord in such a way that all of the invited guests can sit down together and break bread in fellowship. Similarly to his foundational words in Ephesians, "There is one body and one Spirit, just as also you were called in one hope of your calling; one Lord, one faith, one baptism, one God and Father of all who is over all and through all and in all," (Ephesians 4:4-5), Paul presents the idea that Christian formation and unity begin in worship. The community itself is formed when believers worship together. It breaks down personal and cultural barriers, if we will *set our minds and hearts* on things above and focus on God, by giving ourselves to Him. There is no more distinct way to do this than in loving one another. Since Paul's listeners were not quite there yet, Paul led them by getting them started in worship, lifting high the name of Jesus. And, as Paul explained, "Christians are to adjust their way of thinking about everything in accordance with the 'newness' of their life in the Spirit (cf. Romans 7:6).[115]

The content and prime characteristic of new life in the Spirit for the believer is the self-giving love demonstrated by Jesus. This kind of love is both for individuals and for the whole church body and should be lived out in community "both within and outside of the Christian fellowship."[116]   What Paul is communicating in this chapter echoes Jesus' teachings found in the Sermon on the Mount.

12 Therefore, I exhort you, brothers and sisters, in view of God's compassion, to offer your bodies as a living, holy, and pleasing sacrifice to God, your true worship, [2]not conforming to the model of this age. But, be transformed by the renewing of your mind for determining what the will of God is—the good, pleasing and perfect.

A. Love Expressed as Worship (12:1-2)

Worship is grounded in God's compassion (12:1). It takes communion. It takes commitment. "True worship is the offering to God of one's body, and...*is the offering of everyday life to him.*"[117] Paul detailed through Romans that grace is the enabler. Faith and trusting God in Christ is the action people must take.

People become living sacrifices by devoting their entire self to the loving service of others in the name of Christ.[118] In God's own self interaction, one of the prominent characteristics is mutual submission; think *perichoresis*. Humans in relation to God are to submit to God's holy love. Thus, God's presence and power transform us, changing us from one degree of glory into another (2 Corinthians 3:18), becoming more like Jesus Christ. The Christian who becomes "a living sacrifice" acknowledges the Lordship of Christ, personally in the inner life and in the larger Christian community.

This process is a restructuring work of God, moving the believer away from a self-center to a God-center.[119] The point here is not on changing one's outward appearance, combing one's hair differently, or putting on different clothes, but being motivated by a different set of values, being altered at one's core to reflect a change in essence. Not only does this change our focus, but our ethics as well.[120]

Our ethics reflect personal and social holiness, that is, spiritual growth in the midst of Christian fellowship and accountability. The point is not to be some Roman vestal virgin used in sexual licentiousness, or a victim burned upon an idol altar to Molech. Not at all! The imagery is that of a humble active participant, willing to take on Christ-like qualities, presented to God, and available for continuing God's mission in Christ through the ever-present impetus of the Holy Spirit. God is urgently beckoning; a willing and responsive person will find God's compassion filling up their life, and decide to get involved in the lives of needy people for Christ's sake. The guidelines by which we make such decisions, our ethics, are now informed by the love of Christ and His Godly principles.

Right actions will not follow, however, if the mind is not willingly engaged and renewed. The body will not follow righteousness, if the mind is set toward evil. In that sense, an evil mind is worthless, unqualified to assess the truth about God, His will, ourselves, or the world He has made. God's work of transformation is the reverse of the mind-set of worldliness. In the Spirit, we discover the will of God. We can understand it with our mind enough to agree with it and put it into practice.[121] The moral direction Paul affirms is "what is good, acceptable to God, and perfect." Its content and goal is holy love, internally renewed and externally expressed.[122] Again, instead of yielding ourselves to the evil desires of a self-centered world, Paul tells us to "go on being transformed," by embodying the holy, humble, gentle, patient love of God and people.

Righteousness has an active purpose. It is not to look pretty sitting upon a shelf—or in a seat in a church building, as the case may be. Sanctification is not for museum display cases, but for life in the Spirit out *in* the world, and while living, spreading the character of Christ to others. Social holiness leads to social justice: works of piety lead to works of mercy. The unity of the Church and peace in the neighborhood are at stake!

B. Love Expressed in Unity (12:3-13)

³For I say by the grace given me to everyone among you, not to think of yourself more than you ought, but rather think with sober judgment, divided according to the faith God has measured to each of you. ⁴For even as we have one body with many members, and these members do not all have the same function, ⁵thus in Christ the many form one body, and individually members of one another. ⁶Since we have differing grace gifts, according to the grace given to each of us, If prophesying, then prophesy according to the analogy of faith; ⁷if serving, then serve; if a teacher, then teach; ⁸if an exhorter, then in encouragement; if giving, then give generously; if presiding, do it diligently; if one who show mercy, do it gladly.

⁹Love without hypocrisy, abhorring evil; cling to the good. ¹⁰Be devoted to one another in kindred love. Honor one another above yourselves; ¹¹in zeal, be diligent, fervent in the Spirit, serving the Lord, ¹²rejoicing in hope, patient in distress, faithful in prayer, ¹³sharing in common with the saints who are in need. Practice hospitality.

The unity of the Church is a major concern in its own right, but disunity also threatens to impede the spread of the gospel toward people at the margins of society (Romans 10:8). Paul hammered this boldly and, yet, delicately throughout the whole letter thus far. That emphasis will not diminish even when the letter takes up the practical applications of spiritual formation for the Christians at Rome. The force of Paul's argument is that, "The Christian faith and praxis which the Roman Christians share in common should distinguish them from others more than their differences divide them from each other."[123] This work of the Spirit is the shedding of love abroad in the heart and life of the believer as "righteousness, peace and joy in the Holy Spirit!" What we see is the awakening of the "eschatological vision of a community ethic… and situation in which the Spirit of God has been fully poured out, enabling God's people to press on to the 'obedience of faith.'"[124]

One result of this vision is that Christians do not hoard their spiritual gifts (or other belongings for that matter), but give them in service to Christ in the church and the community. Paul mentions the gifts that could be active in their fellowships, to remind them, that such gifts are to care for each other. Spiritual gifts are not for boosting one's ego, but for practical living in a hostile environment. Christians really need to depend on each other. Those with leadership gifts should use them to strengthen and lead the community in zealous love, and selflessness. Although Paul listed a few representative gifts in 12:6-8, this list is not exhaustive, nor is it to indicate a specific structure, but rather highlight that the gifts cooperate. The key to using the gifts correctly is to implement them through love, genuine, sincere love (v.9).[125]

Love increases when we use our spiritual gifts for the benefit of others. Such gifts are not for personal gain, but for strengthening, building up the body of Christ in unity, service, and worship (12:9-13). How a person uses his or her gifts demonstrates who or what is at the center of their life. Paul's instructions teach practical elements of what it means to have "been adopted into the family of God by the power of the Spirit (see 8:12-17)." Paul was not advocating a loss of the individual into some bland group consciousness, but real community that is only attained in the Spirit, and in mutual sharing.[126] Christians are now to conform to their new godly character traits,[127] and be available for kingdom of God efforts. Love stretches out a hand to make what is formed in the mind into a viable, living reality. Love never expressed is not real love; it is only imaginary.

Genuine love takes shape in noticeable ways. This means that for Christians to live up to and live out what Paul is telling them in this letter, the sanctified love in their hearts must demonstrate its real presence through the sharing of their lives. Paul gave them practical examples of love through proper expressions of giving of their possessions, using their personal talents, and God-given spiritual gifts for making the community better. The humble joy, love and hope by which they infect others are unmistakable tell-tale markers of what it means to be a sanctified, spirit-filled follower of Jesus Christ.

C. Love Expressed in the Neighborhood (12:14-15:13)

¹⁴Bless those who persecute you; bless and do not curse. ¹⁵Rejoice with those who rejoice; mourn with those who mourn. ¹⁶Live in one accord with one another. Do not think too highly of yourself, but associating humbly with one another. Do not be conceited. ¹⁷Do not repay evil for evil. Take thought to do what is honorable before everyone. ¹⁸If it is possible, as for your part, be at peace with everyone, ¹⁹not taking revenge, beloved, but leave room for God's wrath, for it is written: "It is mine to avenge; I will repay," says the Lord. ²⁰On the contrary: "If your enemy is hungry, feed him; if thirsty, give him a drink. In doing this, you will heap burning coals on his head." ²¹Do not be conquered by evil, but conquer evil with the good.

In 12:14-21, Paul also guided believers in how they are to get along with their non-Christian environment, which would not always be friendly toward them. Believers are to live in such a way that their inner commitment to Christ is evident in their outward demeanor and behavior (v. 14). Paul is providing practical instruction to help the community establish a deeper sense of *koinonia* where their love

toward Christ is expressed toward those in the civil sphere. This is done in ways that honor Christ, by respecting the humanity of other people, regardless of the other person's intent, even if it is hostile (v. 17).[128] In this way we demonstrate who our Father is.

Thus, the Christian acting under the influence of the Holy Spirit responds in a way that offers our enemies the way of peace and reconciliation (see 5:9-10). The heaping of "burning coals" on the heads of adversaries are acts and words of warm-hearted devotion and love, not revenge and malice in disguise (vv. 20-21)! The point is to turn enmity into friendship, hatred into love, hostility into peace.

"Turning the other cheek" (Luke 6:29-30) is a sign of strength based upon a different set of godly principles. It is not a cowardly bowing to the aggressive will of a domineering bully![129] Paul's admonition here is to express strong Christian character because we belong to Christ. It is not trust in the government, but trust in the supremacy of Christ that guides your actions. You are a person of peace and your interactions convey the *shalom* (wholeness) that you represent for the entire community.

13 Let everyone be subject to the superior authorities, for there is no authority except from God. The authorities that exist have been appointed by God. [2]So that whoever resists the authority is resisting what God has ordered, and those who resist will bring judgment on themselves. [3]For rulers hold no fear for those who do good, but for those who do wrong. Do you want to avoid fear of the one in authority? Then do good works and you will be commended. [4]For they are God's servant for you, for the good. But if you do evil, fear, for rulers do not bear the sword in vain. For he is God's servant, an avenger for wrath against the evil of the wrongdoer. [5]Therefore, it is necessary to submit to the authorities, not only because of wrath but also for conscience sake. [6]This is also why you pay taxes, for the ministers are God's servants, devoting their occupation to governing. [7]Pay to everyone what you owe: If you owe taxes, pay taxes; if customs, then the duties; if respect, then respect; if honor, then honor.

In 13:1-7, Paul was still explaining Christian behavior in our relationship to the wider community. They were in Rome and were subject to the laws of Rome. We should not be focused on these verses as a separate treatise on absolute governmental loyalty. That was not Paul's point and would separate what he says here from the overall intentions of the letter. Christians were not yet being persecuted, but they could become suspect because of their connections to the "rebellious" Jews. Paul was helping them avoid the ire of the imperial administrators.[130]

Paul is reminding the Christians in Rome that their behavior is to reflect well on the Lord. When Jesus was accused of not paying "taxes," or asked about it, He sent money to whom it was due (cf. Mark 12:17).

Paul was raising the stakes of this common argument to the level of stewardship. That is, all things belong to God and all authorities are finally answerable to Him and governed by His principles. If we act in accord to the principle of the "analogy of faith" (12:6), then our action in all things must reflect Christian character acting in faith and faithfulness to Christ, because we are made in the "image" of God. This carries a much greater "stamp" (responsibility and significance) than a physical imprint on any coin.

Paul was undercutting the authority of Rome in an indirect way here as well. He advocated that the real authority in charge is God, whether Rome acts according to godly principles or not is for their vindication or condemnation as a government established for the purpose of limiting evil, keeping the peace, promoting the general common good, and providing order for its citizens under God's true reign.[131] The Imperial cult of Rome would have had trouble with Paul's advice.[132] Just the same, Paul was not rejecting the state when it was operating in a just and fair manner.

Part of what Christians are demonstrating is the influence of grace and the power and presence of the Spirit to transform the spheres of darkness to flood them with light and life that can only come from God. God is alive and active in His people.

Another link to Paul's words of peace with the local community-at-large could be a point of connection to his overall mission of gaining support from the stable Christian population there. This does not suggest some personal, self-serving motive, but a facilitation of the gospel toward Spain and beyond. Although this detail is mentioned specifically only briefly in 15:28-29, it is nonetheless a key element of this apostolic, missionary letter.[133]

∞∞

[8]Owe no obligation, except to love one another. For whoever loves others has fulfilled the law [of Christ].[134] [9]The commandments, "do not commit adultery," "do not murder," "do not steal," "do not covet," and any other command is summed up in this one command: "Love your neighbor as yourself." [10]Love does no evil to a neighbor. Therefore love is the filling full of the Law.

∞∞

In Romans 13:8-10, Paul asserted that "love is the fulfillment of the Law." Here we see the open-endedness of love that calls forth the lover to continue to deepen and grow in the relationship.[135] Love is the motivation for the mission. Love is the main feature backing everything God is doing and figures prominently into every doctrine and argument in the letter. It is God's holy love that inspired and motivated Paul and his travels, because that is precisely God's own nature. Remember, God *is* love. This is why love is the fulfillment of the Law. When love is the governor, the characteristics of Christ come into view and are the evidence of the Spirit-filled life of the believer.

The practical implications here are that the Christian demonstrates what it really means to be a follower of Christ most at this level. It is the personal involvement with those within our sphere of influence that has the potential of doing the most good for Christ's kingdom. This is love in action. The activated Christian aims at doing no harm, and doing all the good possible, to everyone. "Love acts for the good of another."[136] This is how Jesus is the "end of the Law." Christ has taken up into Himself the essence of what was good and holy about the Law and provided for its attainment from the heart by the indwelling Spirit. It is not about keeping rules; it is about deepening a relationship. It is about living in such a way as to keep from offending, or violating the relationship; moreover, it is to do the positive things that make it stronger, deeper, and closer. It is living into the reality of having an "unveiled face" in the presence of God with no fear, only love.

[11]And do this, knowing the present time: The hour has already come for you to awaken from your sleep, for the hour of our salvation is nearer now than when we first believed. [12]The night is far advanced; the day is so near. So then put aside the deeds of darkness and put on the armor/weapons of light. [13]Walk decently, as in the daytime, not in carousing and drunkenness, not in sexual excesses and debauchery, not in jealous dissension. [14]Instead, clothe yourselves with the Lord Jesus Christ, and give forethought about how not to gratify the desires of the flesh.

In Romans 13:11-14, the eschatological age impinges upon the present age and is effecting changes. The New Covenant people, living by love, are those who also are characterized by the light of Christ. This means that we can do God's will on earth like it is done in heaven, if not always in performance, at least by willingness of the heart. The Kingdom, inaugurated at the ascension and enthronement of the resurrected Jesus, is at hand.   As citizens of that world, our earth is in the process of being consummated by the transformation offered in Christ: turning, deliverance, justice, peace.[137] The most prominent feature of this notion is the willingness with which we try to carry out God's desires, not those characteristic of our own selfish, evil desires. The anticipation of Christ's return and grand fulfillment is a sobering reminder to not grow lackadaisical in our walk. Maintaining Christian character ("Put on Christ" 13:14) is a part of that Spirit-filled, Christian love-saturated life of mission. In Paul's view, after all, they were living in the "end times," and this was always a factor in his comments on contemporary living.[138] Because the age to come was already begun in Christ's first coming, all believers, were to reflect the Spirit-saturated character of the coming consummation in their present, everyday lives. Christ was to be living and reigning in the heart of His followers, and that reign should be manifest in their attitudes and actions as defined by Christ-like love. The message has not changed: We still live in the "end times," love still defines us; and we should do all we do with an eye toward His return. Be prepared.

14 Welcome the one whose faith is weak, without quarrels over disputable matters. [2]One person trusts that they can eat anything, but another, whose faith is weak, eats only vegetables. [3]The one who eats everything must not despise the one who does not, and the one who does not eat everything must not judge the one who does, for God has welcomed them. [4]Who are you to judge another's servant? They stand or fall before their own master. But they will stand, for the Lord is able to hold them up.

[5]One person judges one day more sacred than another; another considers every day the same. Let each of them be fully convinced in his own mind. [6]The one observing the day does so to the Lord. The one who eats meat does so to the Lord, for he give thanks to God; and the one abstains does so to the Lord and gives thanks to God. [7]For none of us just lives to ourselves alone, and none of us dies to ourselves alone. [8]If we live, we live to the Lord; and if we die, we die to the Lord. So, whether we live or die, we are the Lord's. [9]For because of this, Christ died and returned to life so that he might be the Lord of both the dead and the living.

[10]But you, why do you judge your brother or sister? Or why do you treat your brother or sister with contempt? For we will all stand before the judgment seat of God,

[11]for it is written: "'As I live,' says the Lord, 'every knee will bow to me; every tongue will confess to God.'" [12]So then, each of us will give an account of ourselves to God.

[13]Therefore let us no longer judge one another. Instead, decide to do this: not to put any stumbling block or temptation in the way of a brother or sister. [14]I am convinced that nothing is unclean in itself, but if anyone regards something as unclean, then for that person it is unclean. [15]If your brother or sister is grieved because of what you eat, you are no longer walking in love. By your eating, do not destroy someone for whom Christ died. [16]Therefore do not let what you know is good for you to be maligned. [17]For the kingdom of God is not a matter of eating and drinking, but of righteousness, peace and joy in the Holy Spirit. [18]On this principle, anyone who serves Christ is pleasing to God and receives human approval. [19]So then we pursue what leads to peace and building up of one another. [20]Do not destroy the work of God on account of food. All food is clean, but it is evil for the person eating with offense. [21]It is good not to eat meat or drink wine or to do anything else that will cause your brother or sister to stumble. [22]So whatever you believe about these things keep between yourself and God. Happy is the one who does not condemn himself by what he approves. [23]But whoever has doubts when they eat is condemned, because their eating is not

from faith. But, everything that is not
from faith is sin.
◇◇

In chapter fourteen, Paul took up another aspect of love as being patient. We can hear echoes of 1 Corinthians 13 again and again as Paul went over the fine details of applying the gospel of unity and love in Christ.

Jesus refused to reject people damaged by life (Matthew 12:20). Neither should we reject a believer because they want to live by certain rules, or without them (14:1-6).[139] Salvation does not depend on rule keeping, but on how these opinions are handled and how they affect the unity of the church (14:7-9)! I can also seriously damage the faith of another brother or sister, and need to be cautious to avoid doing this.

There are more factors in the life of the church than the Jew-Gentile division. Paul understood that wherever there is diversity among people, there is a potential for dispute and separation, especially about trivial matters, but even over matters of importance. In Corinth, Paul had to deal with spiritual gifts causing a division (1 Corinthians 12-13), which he also briefly covered with the Romans. He had dealt with the meat/dietary issue with other Christians in Corinth and gave attention to it here as well.

The weight of Paul's call is on hospitality, forbearance, and charity, avoiding suspicion, hostility, and division. A judgmental attitude is never welcome in the House of God. Please leave it at the door! No matter who it is, that type of arrogance is always out of place and causes grief.[140] To lead a person to go against their conscience is an act of "unfaith" and tears a person down instead of building them up in the faith.[141] If someone is not convinced in his or her own mind, then he or she is not acting in accord with faith/trust. It is a pretense. Paul puts it more bluntly, it is sin (14:23). Shall we cause our brothers and sisters to stumble (14:15)? The point Paul was getting at is not who is more right, "weak" or "strong" Christians. What Paul was rejecting was their rejecting of each other over their opinions! Such rejection destroys the fellowship. The way Paul put it here is that disunity is the greatest threat to the church, not their eating and drinking practices.[142] Although the point is quite serious, you can hear the subtle ironic humor in this type of food war—and unless they are careful, in their "eating and drinking contest," they will devour and consume the fellowship! Would you eat dinner with people that you detest or fear? No, the risk is too great and it is upsetting.

You will not sit down at the banquet table to eat with enemies, too much could happen in that vulnerable setting (i.e. being poisoned, or dropping your guard against an attack). Nor is it pleasant to eat with people with whom you are at odds; it causes indigestion.

At the beginning of this section, Paul lays out the reason for unity, inviting people to join him at the table of fellowship with Christ. At the table of fellowship, where Jesus is the host, people share the common meal as a sign of their oneness in the Lord. Any divisive attitude threatens to disrupt or prevent harmony in their Christian life and hinder God's mission. The critical verse is 14:17, For the *kingdomain* of God is not food and drink but "righteousness and peace and joy in the Holy Spirit." The practical implication is that if there is anything that is "morally indifferent to me, before I act on that conviction, I must consider how that action will affect the peace of the Church and the Christian growth of others."[143] Love, then, is the governor of our actions. Love allows or disallows what we do in regards to our behavior, choices, or freedoms set in the context of the community and our relationship to Christ. What cannot continue is flaunting freedom, or despising and judging one another. Those are clear abuses devoid of Christian content. Paul firmly rejects them both as sin.

Paul did not let up on the theme of unity, but he did turn to bring in another facet. At the start of the chapter, he laid out that the foundation of the believers relationship is in Christ, the Messiah, and the oracles of God are still there for our encouragement.

15 We who are strong ought to bear with the weakness of those without strength and not please ourselves. [2]Each of us should please the neighbor for the good, to build them up, [3]for even Christ did not please himself. But, as it is written, "The reproaches of those who have reproached you have fallen on me." [4]For whatever was written in the past was written for our instruction, so that through patience and the counsel of the Scriptures we might have hope. [5]May the God of patience and counsel give you the same mind toward each other that Christ Jesus had, [6]so that with one mind and one

> voice you may glorify the God and Father
> of our Lord Jesus Christ.

Christianity is not a solitary religion (15:2). It is not just about me and Jesus. In fact, we are to put others ahead of ourselves. We are a community formed around the Christ, and we learn about Christ and the work of God in "former times through what was written for our instruction" illumined by the Holy Spirit to inspire hope in us (15:4). We are a community of faith and our actions affect others. Thus, we should act in a responsible manner according to Christian principles of mutual Christ-like love (15:5). On the one hand, the boundary of our Christian freedom is the good of fellow Christians.[144]   On the other hand, whatever is done in Christian freedom must be honorable to God (15:6). *Love does not violate its relationships.*   Instead, Christian fellowship in love is marked by being considerate.[145]   Paul's melodic appeal is for their symphonic voices intoned in harmony to produce a praise chorus of unified quality, evoking "glory to the God and Father of our Lord Jesus Christ." To do otherwise "diverts precious time and energy from the basic mission: the proclamation of the gospel and the glorifying of God"[146] in, thought, word, and work.

> [7]Therefore, welcome one another as Christ welcomed you, unto the glory of God. [8]For I say that Christ has become a servant of the circumcised for the sake of God's truth, that he might confirm the promises to the patriarchs [9]but, the Gentiles glorify God

for his mercy, as it is written: "Therefore I will praise you among the Gentiles; I will sing the praises of your name." [10]Again, he says, "Rejoice, you Gentiles, with his people." [11]And again, "Praise the Lord, all the nations, and let all the peoples praise him." [12]And again, Isaiah says, "The Root of Jesse will come, and the One who will arise to rule over the nations; in him the nations will hope." [13]May the God of hope fill you with all joy and peace as you trust in him, so that you may abound with hope overflowing by the power of the Holy Spirit.

The work of Christ welcomes both the Jew and the Gentile, any group or designation has an open invitation. Christ came that all may have a seat at His table. He fulfilled the requirements of the Law and the promises to the Jews so that they are not lost even while He rises to extend hope to all the nations (15:7-13). Paul makes one more appeal demonstrating God's intention for the unity of the church in Christ.

In this final exhortation for unity, Paul bases it on the gospel confession from Isaiah calling for faith in the Messiah who God raises. Paul's connection of the old and the new in the God who raised Christ Jesus from the dead and empowered the Church through the sending of the Holy Spirit, for Jewish and Gentile believers alike, would bring to fruition His confident appeal to them to be one in Christ.

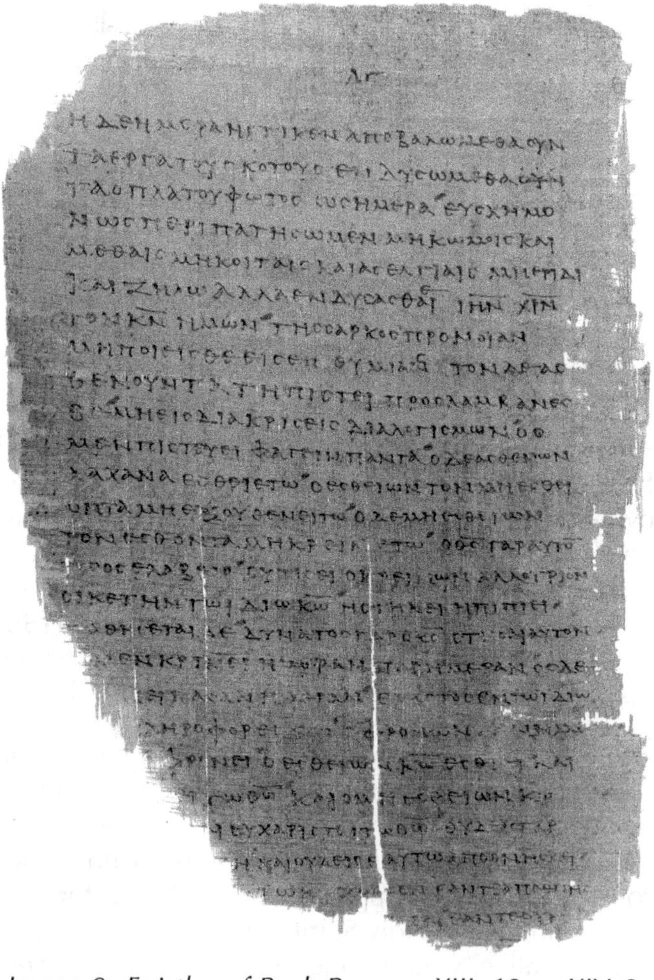

Image 9: Epistles of Paul, Romans XIII, 12 — XIV, 8.

IV. Mission Critical Plans and People (15:14-16:23)

From chapter one, Paul laid the foundation of the church upon the grace of God, manifesting itself in the work of Christ and the outpouring of the Holy Spirit upon believers (Acts 2:4 Jewish; 10:44 Gentile). Paul showed that "the gospel...is God's power leading to salvation to everyone." The Jew and the Gentile are included in God's plan of salvation by grace through faith or trust in Christ offered on an equal basis. He argued that all of God's actions were proven just in his inclusion of all peoples.

It is still God's intention that the Church pull together in love, exhibiting "righteousness, peace, and joy in the Holy Spirit." This newness of spirit, being renewed in the image of God, and based on harmony in fellowship with one another is to characterize the internal character and external actions of followers of Christ. This solidarity in Christ and with one another is an essential testimony to the work of God that is attractive to a needy world who waits for the gospel to reach them.

A. Mission Critical Plans (15:14-33)

◇◇◇

[14]I myself am fully persuaded, my brothers and sisters, that you yourselves are full of goodness, filled with knowledge and competent to train one another. [15]Yet I have written you quite boldly on some points to remind you, because of the grace God has given to me [16]to be a public minister of Christ Jesus to the Gentiles, serving the priestly duty of proclaiming the gospel of God, so that the Gentiles might become an offering acceptable to God, sanctified by the Holy Spirit. [17]Therefore I boast in Christ Jesus in my service to God. [18]I will not dare to speak of anything except what Christ has accomplished through me for the obedience of the Gentiles in word and deed [19]in the power of signs and wonders, in the power of the Spirit of God, with the result that from Jerusalem all the way around to Illyricum, I have fully proclaimed the gospel of Christ, [20]in this way making it my intention to preach the gospel where Christ was not known, in order to avoid building on someone else's

foundation.   [21]But, just as it is written:
"Those to whom it was not told about
him, they will see, and those who have not
heard, they will understand."

◇◇

Paul returned to a theme introduced near the
beginning of the letter, commending the faith and
spiritual growth of Christians in Rome to the point of
being able to teach one another (1:12, 5:14). Here
Paul tagged their spiritual progress and Christian
leadership by connecting their local Christian work
with the larger Gentile mission and Paul's own
apostolic commission (5:16-21). Paul commended
what was good about them while he was acting on
the authority from Christ. He spoke boldly, yet in the
spirit of Christ. It was appropriate to do so in the spirit
and attitude of love and meekness (5:15-16).

The gospel mission of Christ was a vital task of
which Paul would not be idle. He had faithfully
proclaimed Christ throughout the region where
others had not gone. Paul saw this as his primary task
(15:17-20), and founded churches along his journey
from Jerusalem to Illyricum. As he completed his
immediate work, he felt it was time to move in a new
direction (5:21).

◇◇

[22]For this reason I have often been hindered
from coming to you. [23]But now, having
no more place for me in these regions,
and since I have been longing to come to
you for many years, [24]when I go to Spain,
I hope to see you while passing through

and to have you assist me on my journey there, after I have enjoyed your company for a while. ²⁵But now, I am on my way to Jerusalem in the service of the believers there. ²⁶For Macedonia and Achaia were pleased to make a contribution to the poor among the Lord's people in Jerusalem. ²⁷They were pleased to do it, and indeed they are indebted to them, for if the Gentiles have shared in the Jews' spiritual blessings, they owe it to the Jews to share their material blessings with them.

The veteran missionary to the Gentiles finally was headed toward Rome. Paul was excited about seeing what he had heard about the work of God in the capital city (5:22-23). There is an invigorating refreshment of being in the company of other like-minded faithful believers. Paul longed to be with these fellow Christians, not just in spirit across the miles and years, but in person, seeing them face to face (15:23). After all, Christian unity is a central part of the message of the letter being read to them! The encouragement Paul experienced through the continuing mission toward "the ends of the earth" motivated him. Paul wanted to go west, and Spain was in his sights (15:24).

Although Paul joyfully anticipated seeing the Church and sharing the spiritual blessing that God would produce among them, there was a greater matter burning upon his heart. Paul needed to deliver the relief fund for the Jerusalem poor that he had collected from those across the region who gave to help their persecuted brothers and sisters (5:25-26). This was a visible demonstration of love and the unity of the whole church, Jews and Gentiles (15:27)[147] Gently, subtly, Paul was nudging the Romans to be aware of the debt of love that they, too, owed with the rest of the Gentiles. The gospel had come to them by way of the Jews, as well. The Jerusalem Church needed the help and the contributors needed to give to express their gratitude for the gospel coming to them through the lives of the faithful Jewish believers. The implication was that the Romans should be willing to generously join the effort on their "own" initiative (15:25-27).

◇◇

[28]So after I have completed this task and sealed this fruit for them, I will visit you on the way to Spain. [29]I know that when I come to you, I will come in the fullness of the blessing of Christ.

◇◇

Paul indicated that he had the blessing from the Lord to pursue a trek to Spain, and earnestly desired the Roman believers' participation in this endeavor (15:28-29).[148] He knew the dangers of returning to Jerusalem, for there were still those who sought to kill him (cf. 2 Corinthians 11:32-33; Acts 9:23-25).[149] Yet, Paul knew firsthand that God works through prayer. Prayer is not a magic formula that manipulates God into doing what we say. It does not depend on motions, gestures, power words, or even quoting the Bible. Instead, in the humble, submissive heart of the petitioner, the Holy Spirit mingles His words and the will of God with our love and obedience to God and produces a reality compatible with the kingdom and glory of God. Paul knew the power of God. He was

content to live into whatever God was doing. Paul
discerned that through prayer he participated in God's
work in a way that nothing else did or does today. In
prayer, we are the Church, united in Christ and in
His Spirit. Through giving, prayer and mission, Paul
exhorted those who were at odds with one another, to
lay down their opposite opinions and agree on these
more important matters.

> [30]I urge you, brothers and sisters, through
> our Lord Jesus Christ and by the love of the
> Spirit, to go all-out with me in my struggle
> by praying to God for me [31]in order that
> I may be delivered from the disobedient
> in Judea, and that the contribution I take
> to Jerusalem may be favorably received by
> the saints/Lord's people there, [32]so that I
> may come to you with joy, by God's will,
> and I might be refreshed in your company.
> [33]The God of peace be with you all. Amen.

Thus, he asked them to join him in prayer for this
ministry that would signal, the equality of the Gentile
churches with the Jewish church, and the mission that
lay thereafter (5:30-33). In that act of prayer for Paul
and the Jerusalem contribution was the seed for the
healing of the Roman church's divided hearts and
mind. Paul trusted that whatever he would encounter
there, the love of the Spirit would sustain him. But, he
also wanted this to bear fruit among those who read
his letter. Even in asking for prayer for himself, Paul
was demonstrating to them his love for others. This
model leadership, if they emulated it, would also lead

them to more fruitful ministry in the power and love of Christ in the ministrations of the Holy Spirit in their midst.

B. Mission Critical People (16:1-27)

[150]In order for this letter to find a hearing with the believers in Rome, it is likely that Paul selected Phoebe, a trusted leader, in the Corinthian Church, to carry the letter and provide for its reading, either read by her or possibly by a skilled speaker like Paul if Phoebe could not fulfill that role. This was to allow the special emphases and proper emotional tone to be conveyed to them (16:1-2).

◇◇◇

16 I commend to you our sister Phoebe, a deacon of the church in Cenchreae [2]in order that you might welcome her in the Lord in a way worthy of his people and to stand by her in any help she may need from you, for she has been the benefactor of many people, including me.

[3]Greet Prisca and Aquila, my co-workers in Christ Jesus, [4]who risked their necks for my life, for whom not only I, but all the churches of the Gentiles are grateful to them, and [5]greet also the church that meets at their house.

Greet Epaenetus, my beloved, who was the first fruits to Christ in Asia. [6]Greet Mary, who worked very hard for you.

[7]Greet Andronicus and Junia, my fellow Jews who have been in prison with me. They are esteeemed among the apostles, and they were in Christ before me.

[8]Greet Ampliatus, my beloved in the Lord. [9]Greet Urbanus, our co-worker in Christ, and my beloved Stachys. [10]Greet Apelles, with every show of affection who is proved in Christ.

Greet those who belong to the household of Aristobulus. [11]Greet Herodion, my fellow Jew. Greet those in the household of Narcissus who are in the Lord.

[12]Greet Tryphena and Tryphosa, hard workers in the Lord. Greet my beloved Persis, who has worked very hard in the Lord.

[13]Greet Rufus, chosen in the Lord, and his mother, who has been a mother to me, too.

[14]Greet Asyncritus, Phlegon, Hermes, Patrobas, Hermas and the other brothers and sisters with them. [15]Greet Philologus, Julia, Nereus and his sister, and Olympas and all of the Lord's people who are with them. [16]Greet one another with a holy kiss. All of the churches of Christ send greetings.

[17]I urge you, brothers and sisters, to watch out for those who cause divisions and put

obstacles in your way that are contrary to the teaching you have learned; turn away from them. [18]For such people as these are not serving our Lord Christ, but their own appetites, through smooth talk and flattery they deceive the minds of simple people. [19]Everyone has heard about your obedience. I rejoice because of you; but I want you to be wise about what is good, and innocent about what is evil. [20]But the God of peace will soon crush Satan under your feet. The grace of our Lord Jesus be with you.

[21]Timothy, my co-worker, sends his greetings with every show of affection to you, as do Lucius, Jason and Sosipater, my fellow Jews. [22]I, Tertius, who wrote down this letter, greet you in the Lord. [23]Gaius, whose hospitality I and the whole church here enjoy, sends you his greetings. Erastus, who is the city's director of public works, and the brother Quartus send you their greetings.

Paul greeted with warm affection several people who were in Rome and who would be known to the Romans who would support his charge to the church, especially Prisca and Aquila with whom Paul had worked closely. Although Paul had apostolic authority and used it boldly, he did so in ways designed not to offend the hearers or trample on the maturing local Christian leadership. His goal was to strengthen them and advocate an unbreakable bond of love between them all. So he diplomatically mentioned all the names that he could count on to work toward the goals he outlined in the letter.

The hour was late, and the urgency of the mission weighed upon Paul (see 13:11-12).[151] The love in his heart was compelling him to complete his current ministry and carry the flame of God's love into new territory. The transforming power of the gospel had more work ahead, including transforming the work in Rome among the believers!

The gospel is not about instructions, rules, tasks, or accomplishments. It is not about building structures that will stand the test of time as monuments of great achievement. It is about changed lives, being recreated, re-centered, and restructured in Christ. They are the mission. They are where the kingdom of God, as "righteousness, peace and joy in the Holy Spirit" can be seen. The reign of God is about bringing the hearts of his followers into the deep unified fellowship that reflects the characteristics of the Divine Self. This kind of love, then, is to shape their way of life and relationships with everyone. Freedom in Christ is not a scandal to offend, but to bring oneness and wholeness to the body of Christ for the glory of God the Father who is in all, over all, and through all. If the people who are called by his name will humble themselves in this way and seek his face, then they will know all the benefits of heaven in their lives. From that center in Christ, they are called to live and relate to one another in the church and in the community-at-large.

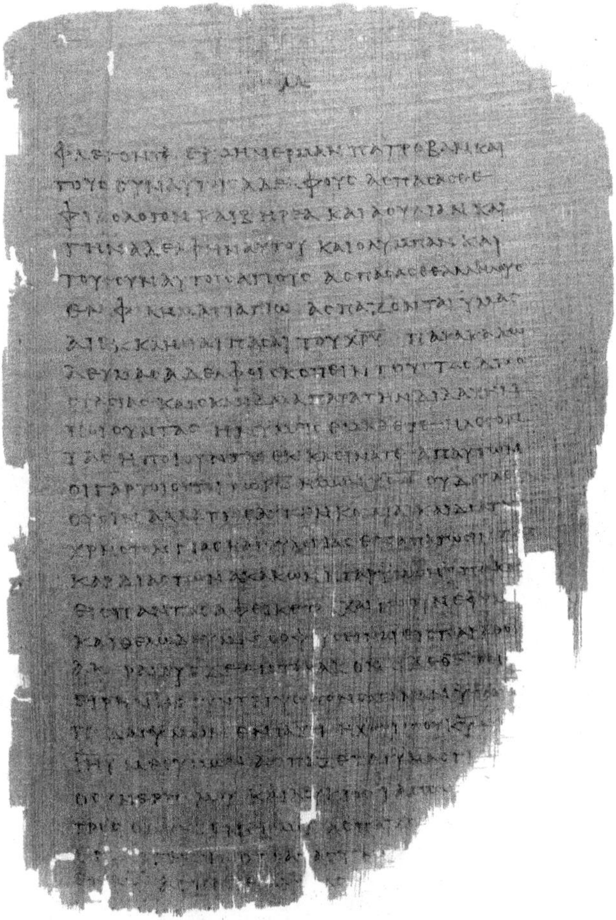

Image 10: Epistles of Paul, Romans XVI, 14 — XVI, 23.

V. Doxological Conclusion (16:25-27)

²⁵Now to him who is able to make you stand you in accordance with my gospel, the preaching of Jesus Christ, in keeping with the revelation of the mystery hidden for long ages past, ²⁶but now revealed and made known through the writings of the prophets by the command of the eternal God, for the obedience of the faith made known to all the nations, ²⁷to the only wise God be glory forever through Jesus Christ! Amen.

"Now to him who is able" provides a closing quotation mark to the letter as it recalls the opening of the letter (cf. Romans 1:1-5, 16-17), concerning the power of God, the gospel, Jesus Christ, the scriptures, the obedience of faith, and all nations.¹⁵² Thus, Paul closed the letter in doxological fashion with the same power and praise theme to God with which it opened: "The gospel and the proclamation of Jesus Christ... now disclosed...to all the nations...to bring about the obedience of faith" (16:25-27). Amen.

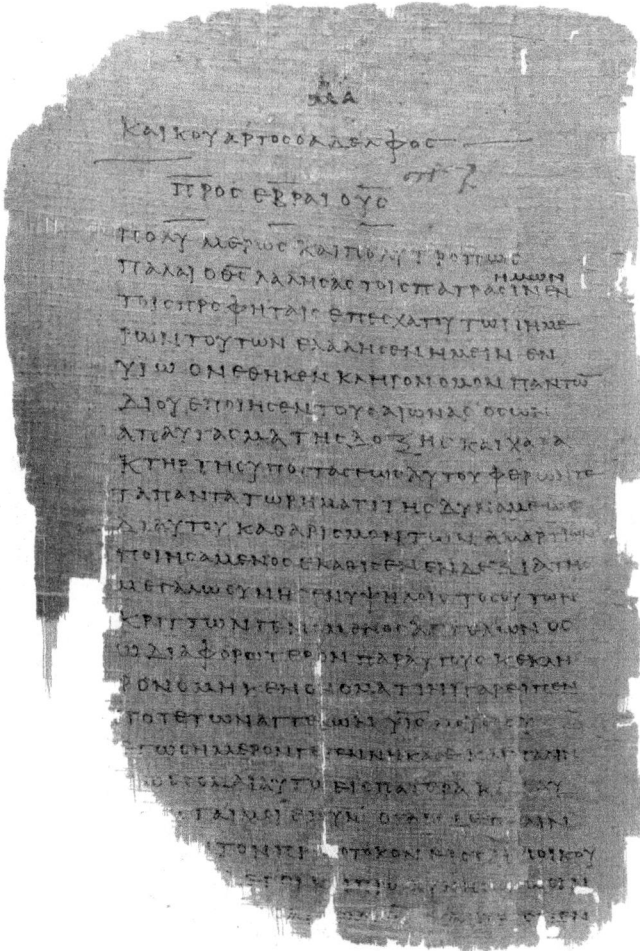

Image 11: Epistles of Paul, Romans XVI, 23 — Hebrews I, 7.

Why Christian Formation Exercises?

Paul gave instructions in this letter on how to live a worthy life. He saw that the goal is a mature attitude, informed and formed by God's characteristics and traits that are evident in the life of Jesus, the perfect human. Therefore, Paul offered to his readers/listeners his best inspired understanding of how that happens to us.

God graciously provides the Way and means to a joyous and holy life. The person who accepts Christ and His ways will discover life's virtues and God's spiritual gifts infused and overflowing in their life. This personal relationship with God, however, is cultivated in one's life in community. We do not live in a vacuum. The intention is that we are a part of something larger than ourselves. We are to be a member of the Church.

The instructions given in the book of Romans give us insight into how we live among others for God, conducting our lives in such a way to create a peaceful, harmonious society, reflecting the godly principles revealed in the Bible. We do not learn everything by ourselves, but with others, being also instructed in the ways of God by His Holy Spirit, who is at work in us and throughout creation.

Paul lays out what God has done for us and what He wants to do in us. His letter to the church in Rome tells us what our role is in how to be a Christian, how to behave, what to expect from other Christians, and what to anticipate from God. This is the purpose for these questions for meditation (careful reflective concentration and prayer) and practice. "Keep your heart." I am responsible for it. This is part of my role. Do I do it alone? No. If I try to do it alone, I will make things worse. Nonetheless, God **enables** me to do my part.

> [3]His divine power has given us everything we need for a godly life through our knowledge of him who called us by his own glory and goodness. [4]Through these he has given us his very great and precious promises, so that through them you may participate in the divine nature, having escaped the corruption in the world caused by evil desires. [5]For this very reason, make every effort to add to your faith goodness; and to goodness, knowledge; [6]and to knowledge, self-control; and to self-control, perseverance; and to perseverance, godliness; [7]and to godliness, mutual affection; and to mutual affection, love. (2 Peter 1:3-7, NIV).

Paul, in Romans 5:5, confirms the progression with these words, "Because the love of God has been poured out within our hearts through the Holy Spirit who was given to us." Again, do I do it alone? Of course not! But, if *I* do **nothing**, it will not be done. In our act, we are cooperating with God and His design and desires for us.

Each of the formation exercises contain the following sections:
1) **Theme**, the subject of the lesson
2) **Read**, the focus scripture passage
3) **Sing**, worship opportunity related to the theme
4) **Reflect,** an idea to think about
5) **Internalize**, questions to apply the passage to your life
6) **Relate**, ways to ally the theme among Christians or the larger world
7) **Prayer**.

As you use these exercises in your own journey, begin by praying this Christian prayer for purity, prayed by millions of Christians worldwide over the centuries to communicate the essence of what we seek:

> Almighty God, unto whom all hearts are open, all desires known, and from whom no secrets are hid. Cleanse the thoughts of our hearts by the inspiration of thy Holy Spirit, that we may perfectly love you, and worthily magnify your holy name, through Christ our Lord. Amen. (The Book of Common Prayer)

Christian Formation Exercises

Learning from Romans

Paul presents his understanding of the gospel of Christ, and apostolic/pastoral admonition concerning the unity of the believers with these themes.

UMH stands for United Methodist Hymnal. CH stands for Celebration Hymnal. If the hymn listed is part of hymnary.org (a listing of words and music to common hymns), then the link is provided.

Exercise I: Encountering the Gospel

Theme: The gospel is God's power leading to salvation to everyone who has faith.

Read: Romans 1:1-17

Sing: "Victory in Jesus" UMH #370

Paul uses the word *gospel* to summarize the life-ministry of Jesus Christ and what it means for the individual, humanity, and all of creation.

Come sinners, to the gospel feast;
Let every soul be Jesu's guest;
Ye need not one be left behind,
For God hath bidden all mankind.

His love is mighty to compel;
His conquering love consent to feel,
Yield to His love's resistless power,
And fight against your God no more.

See Him set forth before your eyes,
That precious, bleeding Sacrifice!
His offered benefits embrace,
And freely now be saved by grace.

This is the time, no more delay!
This is the Lord's accepted day.
Come thou, this moment, at His call,
And live for Him Who died for all.

Sent by my Lord, on you I call;
The invitation is to all:
Come all the world; come, sinner, thou!
All things in Christ are ready now.[153]

Reflect: What do the words *gospel*, *salvation*, and *faith* mean? What do you think is the main purpose of your life?

Internalize: Has the gospel that Paul talks about impacted your life? If not, what does it offer to you? If so, how has your trust in Christ changed your life?

Relate: Find someone this week in the church who will discuss gospel, salvation, and faith with you. Who do you know in the community that needs to hear/experience the gospel?

During your devotional times, pray for that person to encounter the gospel. As you pray, listen to see if God would have you talk with them about it.

Prayer: Lord, use my life as you will to make it so. Amen

Exercise II: God's Fairness and Faithfulness

Theme: The Impartial Righteousness of God that Overturns All Claims of Ethno-superiority.

Read: Romans 1:18-2:16

Sing: "Song for the Nations" CH #439

Paul makes clear that God does not "play favorites." "God shows no partiality" (2:11). Everyone is guilty of sin, but God offers reconciliation to all through Jesus Christ.

Reflect: Paul talks a lot about "the impartial righteousness of God." What does it mean? How inclusive of everyone is it?

Internalize: How does your life display God's righteousness?

Relate: Who do you know that needs to experience God's impartial righteousness? This week, find two people who are different from you and do something kind that they would not expect. If they ask, "Why?" Explain that your act of kindness is one way God shows that no one group of people have exclusive rights to God's love.

Prayer: O Lord, hear my prayers for the whole human race and guide their feet into the way of peace. Purge corruption from your Church, heal her division, and restore her faithful practices. Give grace to our pastors who care for those committed to their care. Bless the leaders of the country with wisdom to lead us in the paths of righteousness for your Name's sake. Keep us, dear Jesus, in constant communion, and humble obedience to you, and, in Christian charity toward one another. Amen

Exercise III: Righteousness Comes through Faith

Theme: Jews and everyone else are put right with God on the same basis.

Like exercise two, this one helps us understand how God works with all of us and each of us. Paul is trying to explain to his fellow Jews and his non-Jewish readers how God works with us to overcome our rebellion, guilt for sinning, and to restore our relationship to God, to each other, to ourselves, and to creation.

Read: Romans 2:17-4:25

Sing: "And Can it Be" UMH #363. http://www.hymnary.org/media/fetch/103440

Reflect: What does Paul mean by sin, the Law, justification, righteousness, grace and faith? What role does God's grace and faith (in Christ) play in your life?

Internalize: How can you have the kind of faith Paul talks about? How does faith that leads to having God's righteousness affect your relationships?

Relate: Talk to someone about your faith this week and tell them how your life is different since you have become a Christian. Ask them about their faith journey.

Prayer: Dear Lord, Redeemer, yet Judge, deliver me from my sins and selfishness this very hour. I have sinned, but gracious, merciful Jesus, you are my advocate. You spilled your blood on my account, so deliver me from the guilt and power of sin that I might rise to serve you now and in your glorious kingdom to come. Amen

Exercise IV: Sanctification: Transforming Your Life

Theme: Life in Christ is the basis of honor that replaces the quest for righteousness through conformity to the Law of Moses.

"Justification is God's proclamation that a person is righteous, and that God makes it so."[154] This change is not only to a right relationship with God, but being set right, an internal, personal, moral change as well. This real change is called sanctification.

Read: Romans 5:1-21

Sing: "O for a Thousand Tongues to Sing" UMH #59 http://www.hymnary.org/media/fetch/96205

Reflect: What is moral change? What does conformity mean? How is your life conforming to Christ? How does the hymn relate to this week's focus?

Internalize: What changes have you noticed in your life and relationship to Christ? What does this initial real change look like in your life? Do you sense a need to deepen your relationships in Christ?

Relate: New life in Christ brings an excitement, a sense of rejuvenation, and the impetus to tell others about what you discovered. Who would benefit this week from your testimony about Christ in your life? Share the hymn with someone who may not have heard it.

Prayer: I will give thanks to you forever and ever, my God, and praise you as long as I have my being. My tongue shall sing of your righteousness and tell of your salvation from day to day. Your power and goodness make me who I am, and I trust you to sanctify me. Praise and thanksgiving are upon my lips because of who you are. Forever and ever will I lift up your Name, O God of my Salvation. Amen

Exercise V: Sanctification: Transformation Continues

Theme: Paul urged the hearers to put behind them their old life in terms of both act and being, and to put on the new life, which is given content by the character of Christ.

Read: Romans 6:1-23

Sing: "It Cleanseth Me" http://www.hymnary.org/hymn/HoC1938/page/71 or "Love Divine, All Loves Excelling" UMH #384 http://www.hymnary.org/media/fetch/97604

Reflect: Why is sin incompatible with the Christian life? Must we continue in sin? Is it possible to stop sinning?

Internalize: What does it mean to die to sin? What role does Christ's death play in our intention to cease sinning?

Relate: Pray for the salvation or sanctification of a family member, friend, or neighbor.

Prayer: Glorious Lord, Jesus Christ, who has brought us out of sin's dark night and made us alive unto God, refresh our hearts with your holy love that we may leave the vanities and the affections of the world behind and set our hearts and minds on you. Amen

Exercise VI: Sanctification: Transformation from What

Theme: Life out from under the legal code.

Paul rejected the base of operation from code-keeping (as misunderstood as the case for righteousness by the Jews, or moral people in general) to love keeping, just as it was intended.

Read: Romans 7:1-25

Sing: "Arise, My Soul, Arise" http://www.hymnary.org/hymn/TH1990/page/322

Reflect: What is meant by the Law? What was life like when trying to live up to those expectations on your own?

Internalize: What is your life like without bondage to sin?

Relate: Pray for those who are still trying to earn God's favor by keeping a code.

Prayer:

> That blessed law of thine,
> *Jesu*, to me impart:
> Thy Spirit's law of life divine,
> O write it in my heart!
> Implant it deep within,
> Whence it may ne'er remove,
> The law of liberty from sin,
> The perfect law of love.[155]

Exercise VII: Sanctification: Transformation by the Spirit

Theme: Life in the Holy Spirit.

Jesus is the demonstration of God's love toward us, and the Spirit in us is the evidence of what is to come. God has mobilized all of the resources of heaven to help every human.

Read: Romans 8:1-39

Sing: "Holiness unto the Lord" http://www.hymnary. org/hymn/J1917/page/71

Reflect: What does it mean to be free from the law of sin and death? What is life in the Spirit?

Internalize: What role does the Holy Spirit play in your life? How does the Spirit bear witness to your spirit that you are a child of God? Do you see the fruit of the spirit in your life? What is the Spirit's role and place in your church?

Relate: Rest in God's love and reliance upon the Holy Spirit each day this week. Talk to two people about the Holy Spirit's work in their life and how they see evidence of the Spirit at work in the church. Pray for the persecuted church.

Prayer: O Spirit Divine, apply the work of Christ to us today. We lift up our brothers and sisters around the globe who are being opposed and hurt by the enemy of our souls and his followers. May they be more than conquerors today. Let us feel your love and spiritual senses enlivened and discern between god and evil through our day. As you inspire us with these desires, so also accompany them with your grace. By your tender mercies let your compassion for others grow in our hearts and be shown to all those within our spheres of influence. Amen

Exercise VIII: God is Trustworthy

Theme: The Triumph of God's Righteousness in the Gospel's Mission to Israel and the Gentiles.

Paul emphasized that the continuity of the Jews was still an integral part of God's continuing plan to reach all people with the message of reconciliation. The history of Israel shows that the rebellious among them or among their neighbors faced equal treatment. That is, trust the LORD, receive His mercy, and live. Serve idols, rejecting God, incur God's wrath, and die. God is consistently trustworthy.

Read: Romans 9:1-11:36

Sing: "I Want a Principle Within" UMH #410 http://www.hymnary.org/text/i_want_a_principle_within

Reflect: Why was it important for Paul to show that God was faithful to the Jews? What would it imply to non-Jews?

Internalize: What does God's faithfulness mean to you? How does God's faithfulness affect your life?

Relate: In a church meeting or in a small group, give a brief description of your story of coming to Christ. Explain what role God's faithfulness played in it.

Prayer: O Lord, let your compassion engulf the whole human race. Enlighten us with your truth; your Word is Truth! Bring your ancient people, the Jews, under the sway of your gospel Be merciful to those in distress, impoverished, and friendless. Christ have mercy. Amen

Exercise IX: Sanctification – All for Jesus

Theme: The personal and collective consecration to God.

Genuine love holds nothing in reserve. It gives the whole self.

Read: Romans 12:1-15:13

Sing: "All for Jesus" CH #588 http://www.hymnary. org/hymn/CEL/page/567 and "Glorious Freedom" http://www.hymnary.org/media/fetch/87954

Reflect: What does it mean to belong totally to God, "a living sacrifice"? How is this expressed in/ as worship?

Internalize: Why is this so important? How is this evident in your life? What are your spiritual gifts? How has God been using you and these gifts for the work of ministry among believers? Out in the community?

Relate: How is this evident in the life of your local Christian fellowship? Give examples. How does your church use its spiritual gifts to serve in the community?

Prayer: O God, who has provided us with all things necessary for life and our salvation, accept our living sacrifice to you and renew our minds from this hour. Fill our hearts with your love that we will be able to live a blameless life before you and a watching world. May your Church be free from scandal, and live in purity and kindness that your Name will be praised and adored among the nations. Amen

Exercise X: Unity in Christ

Theme: Paul's Mission and Travel Plans with an Eye on Global Transformation.

Paul was asking people to participate in his mission to Spain. He recognized that unity is essential to mission. Thus, a primary emphasis in Romans is unity among Christians.

Read: Romans 15:14-33

Sing: "O for a Heart to Praise My God" UMH #417 http://www.hymnary.org/media/fetch/138431 and "A Charge to Keep I Have" UMH #413 http://www.hymnary.org/media/fetch/103660

Reflect: How does unity/disunity affect the goal of personal/corporate transformation to be like Christ? Think about what it means to have a call of God on your life?

Internalize: How does this affect your own life and ability to be a faithful Christian? In what ways are you supporting the mission of God today? Could God be calling you to cross-cultural ministry?

Relate: How does unity affect the spirit at church? How does unity affect the mission of the church? Who gets involved? Pray about participating in a project or ministry at your church that you have not been involved with before to explore if God may be leading you into new territory.

Prayer: Gracious God, Let the inspiration of the Holy Spirit go before me and pour into our hearts a true unity in Christ. Rule in our hearts without a rival. Prosper the work of all those who are engaged in spreading and promoting your true faith and love. May all the peoples and the people of the earth come to Jesus that your great Name, O Father, might be praised among the nations, now and forever. Amen

Benediction

Perfect Love
Perfect Love, how can it be
I worked, I strove, but did not achieve?
By grace through faith, I did believe
Perfect love, now came to me.

Love alone designed Jesus' creed:
Righteous love, life! Full and free—
Holiness met my heartfelt need

Father's Perfect love,
Sent the Holy Dove
To heal our blight
And end our plight.

In mercy, peace and justice win.
Perfect love's victory refrain:
In Christ, we are whole again.
Perfect love won over the din!

Perfect love, how can it be
The seeking God found out me?
God and I are reconciled;
God redeemed the wayward child.

—R. Jeffrey Hiatt

Notes

1. Edwards, 1013.

2. The Blue Letter Bible, "The Epistle to the Romans."

3. Geisler, and William, 294. Accepting Pauline authorship, this letter was either cited or alluded to by: Clement of Rome (ca. AD 95-97), Polycarp (ca. 110-150), the Didache (ca. 120-150), Justin Martyr (ca. 150-155), Tertullian (ca. 150-220), and Origen (ca. 185-254); recognized as authentic by Irenaeus (ca. 130-202), Clement of Alexandria (ca. 150-215), Cyril of Jerusalem (ca. 315-386), Eusebius (ca. 325-340), Jerome (ca. 340-420), and Augustine (ca. 400); and included in the canons of Marcion (ca. 140), Muratorian (ca. 170), Barococcio (ca. 206), Apostolic (ca. 300), Cheltenham (ca. 360), and Athanasius (367).

4. See Acts 18:7; 1 Corinthians 1:14 connecting this leader to Corinth. The Port of Cenchreae (Romans 16:1) is in Corinth; others associated with the Jerusalem relief mission (Acts 10:3-4) were to meet in Corinth, before going to Jerusalem.

5. Jewett, *Romans*, 21-22.

6. Moo, 935f.

7. Prisca is the more formal name of Priscilla. Priscilla would be considered a nickname.

8.   Jewett, 19.

9.   Moo, 5.

10. Witherington, 6. "When we take into account that the letter was written before Paul took the collection to Jerusalem (15:23-28), it was written after Corinthians letters, that it was written from Corinth, prominent Corinthians were mentioned, and Phoebe is the letter bearer, all point to [the selection of this date] (cf. Acts 15:25; 20:2ff)."

11. Moo, 26. In fact, the Law is given an entire segment (Chap. 7) and prominence throughout the letter (cf., e.g., 2:12-16; 4:13-15; 5:13-14, 20; 6:14-15, 8:2-4; 9:31-10:5; 13:8-10).

12. Moo, 17.

13. Jewett, Romans, 75.

14. Witherington, 25.

15. Jewett, Romans, 44.

16. Moo, 39.

17. Moo, 25. Note the phrase "through Jesus Christ our Lord," especially.

18. Snyder, "Misplacing Romans: John Wesley and Hermeneutics."

19. Talbert, "Book Review: Romans: a Commentary."

20. I am influenced by William Greathouse and the Beacon Bible Commentary series for this part of the structural emphasis.

21. Moo, 91.

22. Moo, 93.

23. Greathouse, 50.

24. Greathouse, 55-56.

25. Greathouse, 59.

26. Barclay, "The Letter to the Romans," 40.

27. Moo, 93.

28. Dunn, Romans 1-8, 77-93.

29. Greathouse, 64.

30. Witherington, 91. Paul used the diatribe method of asking a question or raising an issue with a dialog partner so he could answer the question, or respond to the statement.

31. Wright, Vol. 1, 43.

32. Wright, Vol. 1, 47.

33. Achtemeier, 64.

34. See Psalm 14:3 for Paul's reference.

35. Moo, 198.

36. Dunn, Romans 1-8,164.

37. Witherington, 106.

38. Johnson, 52.

39. Greathouse, 87.

40. Grieb, 35.

41. Witherington, 113.

42. Reckoned means that it was credited to him.

43. Achtemeier, 77.

44. Achtemeier, 78.

45. Johnson, 74.

46. Johnson, 74.

47. Johnson, 74.

48. Achtemeier, 85.

49. Dunning, 347.

50. Grieb, 54.

51. Jewett, *Romans*, 80-81; Moo, 290.

52. Witherington, 129.

53. Dunning, 347.

54. Barcaly, 72.

55. Johnson, 83.

56. Achtemeier, 92.

57. Dunning, 341.

58. Dunning, 351, using Ephesians 4:15, quoted by John Wesley in sermon 85, "On Working Out Our Own Salvation," 204.

59. Dunning 474.

60. Dunning 545.

61. Furnish, 172.

62. Wesley, Charles, "O For a Thousand Tongues to Sing."

63. Barrett, 121.

64. Wesley, John, "On Working Out Our Own Salvation."

65. See I Thessalonians 5:23-24; 2 Corinthians 6:14-7:1; 1 Corinthians 2:14-3:4; Colossians 2:8-3:15 which all use the indicative and imperative interplay to lead to this reality in the life of the believer through the work of Christ and the indwelling Holy Spirit.

66. Barclay, 93.

67. Witherington, 179. This technique requires that a speech be given that is "fitting, suiting the situation and character of the one speaking."

68. Witherington, 173. See also 1 Thessalonians 4:3-7 as a parallel passage.

69. Witherington, 181.

70. Even if we conclude that his change in verb tenses allows this section also to be autobiographical, it does so precisely at this point of "everyman" in the same predicament as Adam. (As his own experience as a Pharisee type of law-keeper, he was aware of what was needful—he was instructed by the Law. But, even if one can keep all the outward elements, the inward, spiritual requirements are transgressed. Paul saw what the Law requires, but as one who encounters the Law (or "principles) of God under the sway of sin—which is, the plight of all members of fallen humanity—he fails to do God's will because his heart is not changed.) It includes the Gentile "moralist" of all cultures. It can even include Christians who slip back into a legalistic attitude toward God, as is potentially an ever present danger. No one is excluded from this point of pride.

71. Achtemeier, 130.

72. Witherington, 210.

73. Moo, 468.

74. Greathouse, 173.

75. Dunning, 351.

76. Barclay, 92.

77. Dunning, 428.

78. Achtemeier, 133.

79. Wesley, Charles.

80. Moo, 468.

81. Johnson, 134.

82. Achtemeier, 137.

83. Achtemeier, 140.

84. Witherington, 219.

85. Snyder, Salvation Means Creation Healed, xvi

86. Witherington adds this word of caution, "God has a firm loving grip on the believer, and no outside force can separate the believer from God and God's love. A believer cannot lose his or her salvation as one might lose one's glasses. But by willful rebellion there is the possibility of apostasy, of making shipwreck of one's faith. The Good News, then, is that one cannot lose or misplace one's salvation or simply wander away by accident. Indeed, only by an enormous willful effort could one throw it away. Such is the loving grasp God has on his children" (235).

87. Witherington, 245.

88. Moo, 548.

89. Moo, 550.

90. Wesley, John, Romans 9.

91. Witherington, 238.

92. Dunning, 587.

93. Dunning, 512.

94. Witherington, 245, quotes N.T. Wright affirming, "Paul is not writing a post-enlightenment treatise about how all religions are basically the same; nor...an essay on a modified version [that] the one God has made two equally valid covenants, one with Jews and the other with Christians. Nor...a postmodern tract about how everyone must tell their own story and find their own way...Paul does not accommodate himself to our agendas." What Paul insists on is Jesus as Messiah and Lord.

95. Witherington, 253.

96. Remember that there were some Egyptians who went with the Israelites.

97. Dunning, 511

98. Witherington, 249.

99. Moo, 620.

100. Barclay, 134.

101. Witherington, 260.

102. Achtemeier, 168.

103. Moo, 619.

104. Dunning, 265, 440.

105. Achtemeier, 169.

106. Witherington, 261.

107. Barrett, 188.

108. Achtemeier, 171.

109. This is a refutation of dispensationalist views of supersessationism.

110. Wright, Vol. 2, 46-51.

111. Moo, 707.

112. Barclay, 154. This is the meaning of the "Hound of Heaven" poem.

113. Greathouse, 228.

114. Witherington, 277; Achtemeier, 178.

115. Moo, 756-57. He also notes (Romans 7:6-newness of life in the Spirit, Titus 3:5; 2 Corinthians 4:16-"our inner person being renewed day by day"; Colossians 3:10- "renewed in the knowledge and image" of God; Romans 6:4 "newness of life"; Ephesians 4:23- "be renewed in the spirit of your mind") illuminating passages for understanding the depth of what Paul was saying and the work the Spirit is doing in the life of the believer(s).

116. Greathouse, 233.

117. Barclay, 157.

118. Witherington, 284.

119. Achtemeier, 195.

120. Greathouse, 234.

121. Moo, 757

122. Harper. This is sapiential theology. It is theology that is lived, not just believed—an expression of faith, not just a profession of it. The Rule of Benedict is "theology performed"—day in and day out—alone and in community—through worship and work.

123. Witherington, 280.

124. Witherington, 283.

125. Moo, 775 points out, "Christian love is always grounded in and enabled by the love of God expressed in the gift of his Son (see John 13:34; 1 John 4:9-11)." Note Jesus' affirmation in Mark 12:28-34. Love is a necessity; it is an indispensable mark of the "new creation" in Christ Jesus.

126. Dunn, Romans 9-16, 723.

127. Achtemeier, 196.

128. Witherington, 291.

129. Think Cowardly Lion vs. Wicked Witch in the Wizard of Oz.

130. Witherington, 305.

131. Achtemeier, 205.

132. Witherington, 307 is reflecting R. Jewett in "Response: Exegetical Support from Romans and Other Letters," pp. 58-71.

133. Jewett, Romans, 75.

134. Although the actual words "in Christ" are not in the text, whatever way you read the word other, whether it is taken with the word person, or goes with the word Law, the intent of the message is that In Christ governs the situation. Love covers both areas, making our actions toward others or the essence of the Law as a matter of the heart completed by, in, and through the work of Christ in us.

135. Dunning, 488.

136. Achtemeier, 209.

137. Witherington, 321.

138. Achtemeier, 211.

139. Witherington, 333.

140. Achtemeier, 215.

141. Dunning, 286-287.

142. Achtemeier, 216.

143. Greathouse, 263.

144. Achtemeier, 221.

145. Barclay, 195.

146. Moo, 872.

147. Barclay, 205; Moo, 902.

148. Grieb, 140.

149. Achtemeier, 229.

150. 16:24 is not included in most manuscripts and is considered a later addition.

151. Grieb, 139.

152. Wesley, John, Romans 16.

153. *The Works of John Wesley*, 81-82. The structure of this hymn has been modified from the original hymn, omitting or moving stanzas for emphasis.

154. Dunning, 347.

155. *The Works of John Wesley*, 488.

Works Cited

Achtemeier, Paul J. *Romans,* Interpretation, a Bible Commentary for Teaching and Preaching. Louisville: John Knox Press, 1985.

Barclay, William. "The Letter to the Romans." In *The Daily Study Bible*, 40. Philadelphia: Westminster Press, 1975.

Barrett, C. K. *A Commentary on the Epistle to the Romans,* Harper's New Testament Commentaries. New York: Harper & Row, 1957.

The Blue Letter Bible. *The Epistle to the Romans.* August 1, 2002. http://www.blueletterbible.org/study/intros/romans.cfm (accessed February 15, 2013).

Celebration Hymnal: Songs and Hymns for Worship. Word Music/Integrity Music, 1997.

Dunn, James D. G. *Romans. 1-8,* World Bible Commentary. Vol. 38A. Dallas: Word Books, 1988.

_____. *Romans. 9-16,* World Biblical Commentary. Vol. 38B. Dallas: Word Books, 1988.

Dunning, H. Ray. *Grace, Faith, and Holiness: A Wesleyan Systematic Theology.* Kansas City: Beacon Hill Press of Kansas City, 1988.

Edwards, R. B., and M. Reasoner. "Rome: Overview." In *Dictionary of New Testament Background*, edited by Craig A. Evans and Stanley E. Porter, 1010-1018. Downers Grove, IL: InterVarsity Press, 2000.

Episcopal Church. *The Book of Common Prayer.* New York: Church Publishing Incorporated, 2007. http://www.episcopalchurch.org/sites/default/files/downloads/book_of_common_prayer.pdf (accessed January 23, 2014)

Furnish, Victor Paul. *Theology and Ethics in Paul.* Nashville: Abingdon Press, 1968.

Geisler, Normal L., and William E. Nix. *A General Introduction to the Bible.* Chicago: Moody Press, 1968.

Greathouse, William M. *Romans.* Vol. VIII, in *Romans, I and II Corinthians,* Beacon Bible Commentary. Kansas City: Beacon Hill Press of Kansas City, 1968.

Grieb, Katherine. *The Story of Romans: A Narrative Defense of God's Righteousness.* Louixville, KY: Westminster John Knox Press, 2002.

Harper, Steven. *Benedict's Rule: Sapiential Theology.* January 11, 2013. http://oboedire.wordpress.com/2013/01/11/benedicts-rule-sapiential-theology/ (accessed January 13, 2014).

Jewett, Robert, "Response: Exegetical Support from Romans and Other Letters." In *Paul and Politics: Ekklesia, Israel, Imperium, Interpretation,* edited by Richard A. Horsley, 58-71. Harrisburg, PA: Trinity Press International, 2000.

Jewett, Robert, and D. Kotansky Roy. *Romans: A Commentary,* Hermeneia, A Critical and Historical Commentary on the Bible. Edited by Eldon Jay Epp. Minneapolis: Fortress Press, 2007.

Johnson, Luke Timothy. *Reading Romans: A Literary and Theological Commentary,* Reading the New Testament Series. New York: Crossroad Pub., 1997.

Moo, Douglas J. *The Epistle to the Romans,* New International Commentary on the New Testament. Grand Rapids: W.B. Eerdmans Pub. Co., 1996.

NIV, The Holy Bible, New International Version. Biblica, Inc., 1973, 1978, 1984, 2011. Used by Permission.

Snyder, Howard A. *Misplacing Romans: John Wesley and Hermeneutics.* March 8, 2013. http://howardsnyder.seedbed.com/2013/03/08/misplacing-romans-john-wesley-hermeneutical-corrective/ (accessed January 10, 2014).

_____. *Salvation Means Creation Healed: The Ecology of Sin and Grace.* Eugene, OR: Cascade Books, 2011.

Talbert, Charles H. "Book Review: Romans: A Commentary." *Interpretation: A Journal of Bible and Theology* (http://int.sagepub.com/content/62/2/194.full.pdf+html) 62, no. 2 (2008): 194-196.

United Methodist Church. *The United Methodist Hymnal: Book of United Methodist Worship.* Nashville: United Methodist Pub. House, 1990, 1989.

Wesley, Charles. *O For a Thousand Tongues to Sing.* January 18, 2013. http://www.cyberhymnal.org/htm/o/f/o/ofor1000.htm (accessed March 15, 2013).

Wesley, John. "On Working Out our Own Salvation, Sermon 85." In *The Works of John Wesley Volme 3: Sermons III (71-114)*, by Albert C. Outler. Nashville: Abingdon Press, 1986.

_____. "Romans 9." *John Wesley's Explanatory Notes.* http://www.biblestudytools.com/commentaries/ wesleys-explanatory-notes/romans/romans-9.html (accessed March 17, 2013).

_____. "Romans 16." *John Wesley's Explanatory Notes.* http://www.biblestudytools.com/commentaries/ wesleys-explanatory-notes/romans/romans-16. html (accessed March 18, 2013).

_____. *The Works of John Wesley: A Collection of Hymns for the use of the People called Methodists.* Bicentennial Edition. Edited by Franz Hildebrandt, Oliver A. Beckerlegge and Ddale James. Vol. 7. 24 vols. Nashville: Abingdon Press, 1983.

Witherington, III, Ben, and Darlene Hyatt. *Paul's letter to the Romans: A Socio-Rhetorical Commentary.* Grand Rapids: W.B. Eerdmans Pub. Co., 2004.

Wright, N. T. *Romans Chapter 1-8*, Paul for Everyone. Vol. 1. Louisville, KY: Westminster John Knox Press, 2004.

_____. *Romans Chapter 9-16*, Paul for Everyone. Vol. 2. Louisville, KY: Westminster John Knox Press, 2004.

Images Cited

These images have been turned to gray scale and modified slightly for print and eReader formats. To view the original images, in color, please visit the website in the citation.

Image 1 on page 2: "Papyri p10 Romans 1:1-7." *Early Bible.* http://www.earlybible.com/manuscripts/p10.html (accessed January 21, 2014). Image in the public domain.

Image 2 on page 4: Boulogne, de, Valentin. "Saint Paul Writing His Epistles." *Wikipedia.* January 4, 2013. http://en.wikipedia.org/wiki/File:Probably_Valentin_de_Boulogne_-_Saint_Paul_Writing_His_Epistles_-_Google_Art_Project.jpg (accessed January 21, 2014). Image in the public domain.

Image 3 on page 6: "Overview of Geography Relevant to Paul of Tarsus." *Wikipedia.* December 11, 2012. http://en.wikipedia.org/wiki/File:Broad_overview_of_geography_relevant_to_paul_of_tarsus.png (accessed January 21, 2014). This file is licensed under the Creative Commons Attribution-Share Alike 3.0 Unported license.

Image 4 on page 12: Asbury Theological Seminary Archives. "Acts 28:25-31 and Romans 1:1-9 1598 Geneva Bible." ePlace Images From the Archives. http://place.asburyseminary.edu/fromthearchives/3/ (accessed February 20, 2014). Image in the public domain.

Image 5 on page 14: Asbury Theological Seminary Archives. "Romans 1:1-1:28, Codex Vaticanus B." ePlace Images From the Archives. http://place.asburyseminary.edu/fromthearchives/6/ (accessed July 10, 2014). Image in the public domain.

Image 6 on page 19: "Papyri p26 Romans 1:1-10." *Early Bible.* http://www.earlybible.com/manuscripts/p26.html (accessed January 22, 2014). Image in the public domain.

Image 7 on page 61: Rubiëv, Andrel. "Heilige Dreifaltigkeit." *Wikipedia.* May 21, 2005. http://en.wikipedia.org/wiki/File:Andrej_Rubl%C3%ABv_001.jpg (accessed January 21, 2014). Image in the public domain.

Image 8 on page 84: "Epistles of Paul, Romans XI, 36 — XII, 8." *P.Mich.inv. 6238; Recto.* University of Michigan Library Digital Collections. http://quod.lib.umich.edu/a/apis/x-3553/6238_30.tif (accessed January 21, 2014). Image digitally reproduced with permission.

Image 9 on page 106: "Epistles of Paul, Romans XIII, 12 — XIV, 8." *P.Mich.inv. 6238; Recto.* University of Michigan Library Digital Collections. http://quod.lib.umich.edu/a/apis/x-3556/6238_33.tif (accessed January 21, 2014). Image digitally reproduced with permission.

Image 10 on page 117: "Epistles of Paul, Romans XVI, 14
— XVI, 23." *P.Mich.inv. 6238; Recto.* University
of Michigan Library Digital Collections. http://
quod.lib.umich.edu/a/apis/x-3569/6238_40.
tif (accessed January 21, 2014). Image digitally
reproduced with permission.

Image 11 on page 119: "Epistles of Paul, XVI, 23 —
Hebrews I, 7." *P.Mich.inv. 6238; Recto.* University
of Michigan Library Digital Collections. http://
quod.lib.umich.edu/a/apis/x-3570/6238_41.
tif (accessed January 21, 2014). Image digitally
reproduced with permission.

www.ingramcontent.com/pod-product-compliance
Lightning Source LLC
Chambersburg PA
CBHW050125280326
41933CB00010B/1246